CAN WORKING FAMILIES EVER WIN?

"New Democracy Forum operates at a level of literacy and responsibility which is all too rare in our time." —John Kenneth Galbraith

CAN WORKING FAMILIES
EVER WIN?

JODY HEYMANN

EDITED BY JOSHUA COHEN AND JOEL ROGERS
FOR *BOSTON REVIEW*

HD
8072.5

. C36
2002

BEACON PRESS
BOSTON

BEACON PRESS
25 Beacon Street
Boston, Massachusetts 02108-2892
www.beacon.org

Beacon Press books
are published under the auspices of
the Unitarian Universalist Association of Congregations.

06 05 04 03 02   8 7 6 5 4 3 2 1

This book is printed on acid-free paper that meets the uncoated paper
ANSI/NISO specifications for permanence as revised in 1992.

Composition by Wilsted & Taylor Publishing Services

Library of Congress Cataloging-in-Publication Data
Can working families ever win? / Jody Heymann . . . [et al.] ;
edited by Joshua Cohen and Joel Rogers for Boston review.
        p.   cm. — (New democracy forum)
    ISBN 0-8070-0453-7 (pbk. : alk. paper)
    1. Working poor—United States.   2. Working poor—Government policy—
United States.   3. Wages—United States.   I. Heymann, Jody   II. Cohen,
Joshua   III. Rogers, Joel. Series.
    HD8072.5 .C36 2002
    305.5′62′0973—dc21

                                                            2002002446

CONTENTS

3

EDITORS' PREFACE

JOSHUA COHEN AND JOEL ROGERS

Among the saddest stories to have emerged from the Enron scandal are those told by former employees, suddenly dismissed from jobs, now despairing about how they will meet their children's educational and health needs. These stories reveal a dimension of cruel corporate indifference alongside the sheer greed and corruption that have dominated public discussion of Enron. But the enduring American scandal lies not in these personal dramas, but in the fact that literally millions of working parents face comparable uncertainty and fear every day, as they try to balance the demands of work and family. They are not in the headlines, but they are at the center of this New Democracy Forum.

In the lead essay, Jody Heymann argues that the American system of caregiving—of providing support for children and the elderly—has never adjusted to the realities of a modern economy in which most parents work outside the home. Even under the best of circumstances, conflicts between the demands of jobs and those of families are hard to reconcile. But the conflicts for low-income families are especially severe, with deeply disturbing results for children's health and educational attainment. By imposing these special burdens on poorer families, the current system of work and family betrays the ideal of equal opportunity. Heymann has some ideas about how public policy might remedy the unfairness—by providing parents with more time and resources, and schools (including preschools and after-school programs) with the support they need to ensure fair range of opportunities for all.

The respondents raise searching questions about the meaning of equality of opportunity, about the political hurdles to implementing a demanding work-family program, and about whether Heymann's proposals are best suited to advancing her declared goal of equal chances for all. But there is broad agreement that current policy is a disgrace, that remedies are available, and that those remedies will require imaginative and constructive public action: a scarce commodity, even after Enron.

1

CAN WORKING FAMILIES EVER WIN?

JODY HEYMANN

As a nation, the United States holds dear the belief that all people have an equal opportunity to grasp the American Dream. If adults work hard, they are supposed to have an equal chance at succeeding. Likewise, children are supposed to have equal chances at succeeding in school and leading healthy and full lives. But too often they don't. The barriers many working poor parents currently face in the United States make it next to impossible for them to succeed at work while caring well for their children. Although our failure as a nation to provide essential supports affects all working parents, that failure has meant that parents living in poverty are less likely to succeed in the workplace and their preschool and school-age children are more likely to lack basic opportunities.

How Did We Get Here?

In the last century and a half, two major transformations altered the makeup of the paid labor force in the United States. The first, the movement of men out of agricultural

{ 3 }

and other home-based work into the paid industrial labor force, began in the 1840s. The second began in earnest a century later when women entered wage and salary jobs in significant numbers.

From the founding of the United States until the mid-1800s, most children were raised in farm families in which both parents worked at home.[1] In 1830, 70 percent of children lived in farm families, and only 15 percent had a wage-earning father.[2] When most adults were working at their homes or on their land, their children and adult family members in need of care were with them, or nearby, as they worked. With the industrial revolution, the number of families with wage-earning fathers began to rise. In the 1880s, for the first time in U.S. history, children were more likely to be raised in a family in which their father earned a wage or salary outside the home and their mother did not than in a family with two parents working on a farm. By 1930, only 30 percent of American children lived in farm families.[3]

In small numbers, women began entering the industrial labor force as early as men did. Although women were among the first Americans to work in factories in the early industrial revolution, unmarried women made up the majority of the female labor force at that time.[4] For women of color, as for white women, single women predominated in early paid labor force participation.[5]

Married women's limited participation in the labor force in the 1800s and early 1900s was neither an accident nor a result of women's choices, but a reflection of labor market structure. Openings for men and women were advertised separately; many jobs barred women and many others explicitly barred married women. Moreover, employers could legally discriminate against women in hiring. It was not until World War II—when large numbers of women were needed to fill the jobs held by men who had gone to war—that a dramatic decline in discrimination against married women occurred in hiring.[6]

Marked changes in the employment of mothers of school-age children began in the 1940s; equally marked changes in the employment of mothers of preschool children began in the 1960s. By 1990, more than 70 percent of children lived in households in which every parent was in the labor force.[7] Changes in labor force participation affected women's lives from ages twenty-five to sixty-five and led to profound shifts in how many women were at home to care for elderly parents as well as young children.

In short, the changes in the labor force in the last 150 years were the result not just of women entering the labor market but of both men and women entering the industrial and postindustrial labor force. The fact that both men and women work is not new. What has changed is the location and conditions of labor for both men and women. With this transformation in the location and nature of labor, families became dependent on wages and salaries for food, clothing, and other essentials. By the end of this revolution, most families no longer had any adult working at home full-time.

When the first adults in American households joined the formal labor market, our communities, states, and federal government recognized that if lone wage earners were injured, lost their jobs, or grew too old or sick to work, their families would lack money for food and clothing. As a result, a series of state and federal programs—worker's compensation, unemployment insurance, and old age and survivor's insurance—were created in the first third of the twentieth century to ensure that families were cared for even if the single wage-earner could no longer work.[8]

The more recent entry into the labor force of a second group of adults (many of whom are also primary caregivers) completed the transformation in how families meet caretaking needs. However, communities, states, and the federal government—in marked contrast to their response to the first dramatic shift in labor—have hardly responded to this second transformation, with its profound implications for the care of children and other dependents.

Little or nothing has been done to answer the critical questions families have been facing now for decades: Who regularly cares for preschool and out-of-school children when all parents work away from home? Who provides routine care for elderly parents who can no longer care for themselves? What happens when children and the elderly get sick and need care at unanticipated times? What happens when children have developmental or educational problems and need an adult's help during work hours?

The marked movement of men and women into the industrial and postindustrial labor force has transformed the United States. But we as a nation have failed to respond, leaving a rapidly widening gap between working families' needs on the one side and the combination of high workplace demands, outdated social institutions, and inadequate public policies on the other. The cost of our country's failure to meet the changing needs of working families is being borne by children and adults alike. This essay aims to provoke discussion of these critical problems. I have limited my focus here to the extent and consequences of the disparities families face in the United States across income groups.[9]

Barriers for Children and Parents

The failure of public and private policies to recognize and adapt so that working parents are in a position to meet the needs of our nation's children is adversely affecting children's chances during the preschool years, at school, and beyond.

Problems in Early Education

When working families find affordable, accessible, and high-quality education and care for their preschool and school-age children, their children fare well. Children who have the opportunity to attend preschool have larger vocabularies and are better readers at age six than their brothers and sisters who have not had the opportunity to attend.[10] Evaluations of quality early childhood programs have shown a wide range of gains for children, including improved achievement test scores, a decreased need for special education services, decreased rates of retention, and higher rates of high school graduation.[11] The problem is that most families cannot find that care. Moreover, many families in the United States simply cannot afford decent early education or care. In all but one state, the average annual cost of having a child in preschool is more than the average annual cost of public college tuition. In many places, preschool costs twice as much as college tuition. For example, sending a four-year-old to preschool in Seattle costs an average of $6,604 per year, whereas college tuition at a public institution costs an average of $3,151 per year.[12]

One option available for low-income families is Head Start, the principal federal program aimed at providing disadvantaged children with early educational opportunities. But Head Start in its current form serves only a small fraction of the needs of children living in poverty. Only half of three- and four-year-olds who qualify for Head Start are able to attend at all. Because of limited funding and slots, the overwhelming majority of those who attend do so less than full time and for only one year, even though most would benefit from attending more. The availability is even more limited for early Head Start, which reaches less than 2 percent of those eligible.[13]

Insufficient Care for School-Age Children

Like early education, a wide range of extended school programs have been shown to improve children's academic achievement across social class.[14] Well-designed after-school programs can enhance the quantity and quality of time spent on homework. The ability to read is at the core of much of elementary, middle, and high school achievement, and after-school programs have been shown to have important effects on reading. A National Academy of Sciences study on preventing reading difficulties confirmed that children who receive extra time and reading instruction beyond the current school day show significant improvements in their academic achievement.[15] Reading performance improves for children already succeeding in school as well as for at-risk children receiving support in after-school programs.[16] Among at-risk youth, aspirations for completing high school also improve when they participate in after-school programs, and youths in after-school programs are less likely both to drop out of school and to be held back. When communities have more structured activities for school-age children, they have fewer students suffering from major problems—including substance abuse and other behavioral and mental health problems.[17] After-school programs have also been shown to lead to a decrease in crime and victimization.[18] This makes sense given that the hours with the highest rates of children and youth committing and falling victim to crimes are on weekdays between 2 and 8 P.M.[19]

Yet, despite their demonstrated importance, affordable, quality programs for school-age children are not widely available. This is in part because, as grossly inadequate as the public and corporate policies regarding preschool children are, they are far more developed than the policies addressing the needs of schoolchildren. Employers who pride themselves on providing benefit packages for working parents typically present maternity leave policies and preschool child care programs as proof, while doing little or nothing for parents of school-age children. Since the federal government has done little more, school-age children's needs have been largely ignored. As a result, many schoolchildren lack access to supervision and care during out-of-school hours.

The lack of out-of-school opportunities affects both low- and middle-income families. According to the U.S. Department of Education, twice as many parents would like to have an after-school program available to their children as have them available.[20] And the situation is getting worse, not better. The General Accounting Office estimates that the demand in some urban areas for out-of-school programs will soon be four times as great as the supply.[21]

Constraints on Parental Time

Parental involvement in different aspects of children's education is an important determinant of how children fare in school.[22] Parental involvement is associated with higher achievement in all levels of primary and secondary education.[23] Parental involvement is associated with children's higher achievement in language and mathematics, improved behavior, greater academic persistence, and lower dropout rates.[24]

Intermittently, working parents are called to take time off from work to meet with teachers, principals, and learning specialists; they need to visit schools and to help guide their children through difficult periods. Across the country, too many parents lack the paid leave and flexibility they need to take time from work to help their children with school problems. Disastrously, those who most need such benefits have the fewest.

In a study I led in 2000, for example, we found that families with a child in the bottom quartile in reading or math were significantly more likely to face working conditions that made it difficult or impossible for the parents to adequately assist their children. Of parents with a child who scored in the bottom quartile on math, more than half at times lacked any kind of paid leave and nearly three-fourths could not consistently rely on flexibility at work to meet with teachers or learning specialists. One out of three found themselves in multiple jeopardy, simultaneously lacking paid vacation leave, sick leave, *and* work flexibility. One in six were not able to be available routinely in the evenings to help with homework.

Families in which a child scored in the bottom quartile in reading were equally constrained by working conditions. More than half of these parents lacked paid leave, and nearly three out of four lacked flexibility they could rely on to meet with schoolteachers and specialists. Furthermore, as in the case of the parents with children scoring in the bottom quartile in math, one in six of the parents with children scoring in the bottom quartile in reading worked evenings, when their children needed their help with academics.

These patterns also held for the parents of children who were at greatest risk: those who had to repeat a grade in school or who had been suspended from school. Four out of ten of these parents found themselves, some or all of the time, lacking both paid leave and flexibility. Nearly one out of five of these parents worked evenings, and one in eight worked nights (most without any choice), when their children needed them most.

In all these cases, poor working conditions disastrously limited the extent to which parents could be available to help children whose education was in trouble. Can the relationship between parental working conditions and children's poor school performance be explained by other factors? Even controlling for differences in family income and in parental education, marital status, and total hours parents worked, the more hours parents had to be away from home after school in the evening, the more likely their children were to test in the bottom quartile on achievement tests. Similarly, after controlling for other differences, parents who had to work at night were still 2.7 times as likely to have a child who had been suspended from school.

Parents have long played an essential role in the health care as well as in the education of their children. When their parents are present, sick children have better vital signs and fewer symptoms; they recover more rapidly from illnesses and injuries.[25] Furthermore, the presence of parents shortens children's hospital stays by 31 percent.[26]

Despite compelling evidence about the value of parents' sharing in their children's health care, little attention has been paid to the factors that influence whether working parents can participate. In a study conducted in Baltimore, we asked young parents a series of questions about the factors that affected their ability to care for children who became sick. Only 42 percent of these parents were able to stay at home when their children were sick on a regular workday. Of those who were able to stay at home with their sick children, more than half said they could do so because they received some type of paid leave. Twenty-nine percent used paid vacation or personal days, 14 percent paid leave designed to care for sick family members, 11 percent their own paid sick leave, 11 percent unpaid leave, and 7 percent flexible working hours. Twenty-one percent used different work benefits on different occasions. Because they had worse working conditions, parents who were single, who were living near or below the poverty level, or who had a high school education or less were significantly less likely to stay at home when their children became sick.

Our research confirmed that the parents who received some type of paid leave were significantly more likely to stay home with their sick children. In fact, the availability of paid leave was the key determinant in these parental choices. After controlling for other relevant factors, those parents who had either sick leave or vacation leave were 5.2 times as likely to care for their sick children as those who did not have such benefits.[27]

Despite the critical need, the majority of parents do not

consistently have paid leave they can use to care for children, and as a result, children are left home alone or sent to school sick.[28]

Unequal Burdens

The toll on children and adults of our nation's inadequate policies is exacerbating the damage done by persistent income inequalities in the United States. While there is no doubt that families across the country, from every ethnic and racial group, middle-income as well as poor, are dramatically affected by the gap between what American institutions provide and what American families need, the poor are affected first and worst. When social institutions fail families, middle-income families have some resources of their own with which they can try, at least for a time, to plug holes in the dike.

Moreover, low-income families more frequently face the worst working conditions. As noted earlier, paid leave and flexibility at work can critically affect a worker's chances of meeting family members' needs while working. Nationally, families in the bottom quartile of income are significantly more likely to lack paid sick leave, paid vacation leave, and flexibility than families in the upper three quartiles of income. Even people who earn just above the median income are less likely than those in the top quartile of income to have paid sick leave, paid vacation leave, or flexibility (see figure 1). At the same time, they are more likely than those

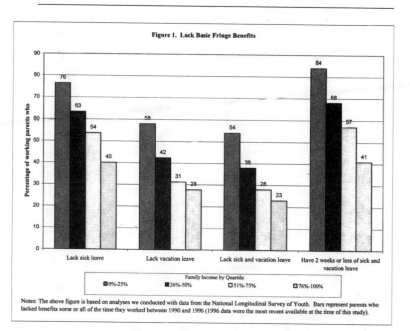

Figure 1. Lack Basic Fringe Benefits

Notes: The above figure is based on analyses we conducted with data from the National Longitudinal Survey of Youth. Bars represent parents who lacked benefits some or all of the time they worked between 1990 and 1996 (1996 data were the most recent available at the time of this study).

in the top quartile to have to work evenings or nights. Among employed parents, 20 percent of those in the lowest income quartile work evenings, compared to 14 and 13 percent of those in the middle quartiles and 7 percent of those in the highest quartile; for night work, the respective figures are 10, 9 (for both middle quartiles), and 6 percent.

On nearly every measure of job flexibility that would enable working adults to care for family members, middle-income employees are worse off than higher-income ones (see figure 2). Furthermore, low-income families face still worse conditions than middle-income ones.

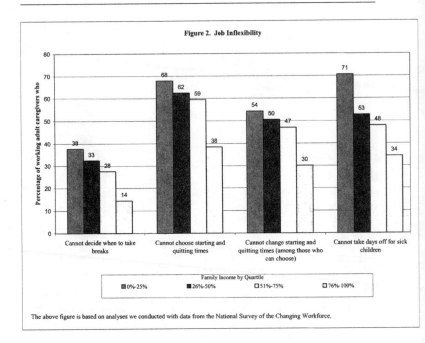

Figure 2. Job Inflexibility

The above figure is based on analyses we conducted with data from the National Survey of the Changing Workforce.

A gradient exists in the need for, as well as availability of, flexible working conditions. Just as they do for children, lower-income working adults have to spend substantially more time caring for elderly parents and parents-in-law by themselves. In fact, families in the bottom income quartile are more than twice as likely as middle- and upper-income families to provide more then thirty hours a month of unpaid assistance to parents or parents-in-law. One of many reasons for this is that lower-income children and adults get sick more often and have more chronic conditions than upper-income ones. Yet fewer lower-income employees have the economic resources to pay for help, and the government provides little support.

EQUAL CHANCES FOR ALL

Failing to respond to the past century and a half's change in the nature of work means that we are failing to meet the essential needs of children and adults in the United States. Moreover, without addressing this failure we won't be able to successfully address inequality. The costly gaps in caregiving do not exist because adults work. The gaps are formed as a result of social conditions that never adapted to the transformation of where and how parents work.

Our society—like any society—must continually reexamine how best to approach at least three essential issues: what values we will uphold, how the work of our society will get done, and how the generations that will lead our country in the future will be raised. The failure to address how working families' needs are met in the United States is affecting all three of these. Our failure to address these needs is profoundly affecting the health, development, and education of children.[29] It is also severely limiting the support available for adults with special health and daily care needs. Furthermore, people who decide to care for children or adults in need face poorer prospects in the workforce because our country allows workplaces to have unnecessary barriers to their meeting both job and family responsibilities. When we discriminate by caregiving status, we diminish the likelihood that adults will take the time to voluntarily provide the care on which our whole society depends.

Basic Job Benefits

Enabling workers to address the fundamental health and safety needs of their families is as important as workplaces addressing the impact of working conditions on the health and safety of employees themselves. We need to ensure that no one has to put the health and welfare of his or her family at risk in order to keep a job.

Although the passage of the 1993 Family and Medical Leave Act (FMLA)—the only federal legislation to directly address any needs of working families in the United States—was an important first step, there are as many holes in the safety net as threads. For those who are covered by the FMLA, the act has safeguarded the possibility of returning to their jobs after unpaid leave for a major illness of a limited number of immediate family members. The value of this leave to those able to use it should never be understated. However, the FMLA fails to provide any coverage to nearly half of American workers, because they work for small employers, have recently changed jobs, or work at multiple part-time jobs to make ends meet. Moreover, three quarters of those covered in theory cannot afford to take unpaid leave and thus receive no coverage in practice. Furthermore, the act provides no coverage for the common illnesses of young children that nonetheless require an adult present, nor does it provide any coverage for educational needs, no matter how great; together these make up the vast majority of children's unpredictable problems. Major illnesses, including terminal ones, of brothers and sisters, parents-in-law, and grandparents are among the many adult needs that remain entirely uncovered.

We should support the ability of Americans to care for themselves and for loved ones in at least two ways. First, short-term paid leave should be available to all working Americans. As documented here, many Americans still have no or only intermittent paid leave. We can afford as a country to ensure that all Americans have at least two weeks of paid family leave, which they can take to meet their own or their family's health needs. This leave should be available for medical visits for preventive as well as curative care. It should be available to meet urgent developmental or educational needs as well: when a child is failing in school and parents need to meet with teachers; when a child is diagnosed with a learning disability and meetings with specialists are required; or when elderly parents are no longer able to care for themselves and need to have essential services arranged. Many companies would not need to increase the leave they already provide. The amount of sick leave they provide would already be sufficient; the only change would be to officially allow it to be used to meet critical needs of family members as well as of the employee. Yet this amount of guaranteed leave would make an enormous difference for those families currently facing the worst conditions.

Second, we need to bring the United States up to global standards when it comes to paid parental leave. More than a hundred countries around the world—from high- to low-income, and with a wide range of political, social, and economic systems—all provide paid maternity leave. Throughout the Organization for Economic Cooperation and Development countries, paid paternity leave is also common. Paid parental leave could be created through many different options, ranging from legislation requiring businesses to provide minimum levels of parental leave to a public insurance system for parental leave that parallels unemployment or disability insurance.

Public Access

Too often left out of discussions about what needs to change so that both work and families can thrive are the civic and social institutions whose practices are grounded, often for no better reason than habit, in the rhythms of a nineteenth-century agrarian economy or in the brief moment during the twentieth century when most households had only one adult in the paid labor force.

For example, in one of the cities the research team I lead has studied, a parent needing to register a child for school had to go in person during the school day to the Parent Information Center, which had no evening or weekend hours.

Making it possible for working parents to register a child for school by mail, let alone by phone, fax, or e-mail—just as they now can register to vote—or offering a wider range of registration times would mean that many parents could handle this responsibility without missing work.

Many private institutions have already made the adjustments. Malls are open in the evening, banks have weekend hours, and grocery stores are open seven days a week. But the gatekeepers for public services and supports for families are often available only from nine to five, or for even more limited hours, Monday through Friday. As in other cases, the barriers are greatest, ironically, for the lowest-income families who most need childcare vouchers, food stamps, WIC, and other public services and supports—and who are also the least likely to have flexible work schedules or paid leave they can take to go to public offices during the workday.[30]

Public transportation provides another example. Because public transportation for children, the elderly, and ill and injured adults is so inadequate, work is often disrupted. Moreover, lack of transportation often keeps families from using available services. For example, while public schools provide bus transportation for the regular school day, even those schools that offer before- and after-school programs commonly fail to provide any transportation for children to support these programs. Similarly, the elderly may have health insurance so they can see a physician but no way to get to their appointments when they cannot drive or walk.

When services of any kind are designed, we need to think

about how children and adults will get to and from those services, given that the majority will come from families in which all working-age adults will be employed outside the home. For some services, this will mean considering distance and location in selecting providers. For other services, we will need to provide public transportation. If we can provide transportation for the regular school day, then we can provide transportation for children in after-school programs. We can no longer ignore transportation issues in the provision of any services for children, the elderly, or the disabled.

Early Educational Opportunities

Although many social institutions need to adapt to these new conditions, the most important changes are required in education. Early childhood education is an important determinant of school performance. Access to such education today looks a lot like access to high school education did in 1949 (see figure 3). In fact, the enrollment rates of children in kindergarten, nursery schools, and other preschools are lower in the United States than in thirteen European countries.[31]

We can afford to do more. In the United States, public expenditures for early childhood education are less than similar public expenditures in Finland, Norway, Austria, the United Kingdom, the Czech Republic, Germany, Italy, and Portugal. Our combined public and private expenditures on early childhood education are a smaller percentage of gross

Figure 3. High School Graduation and Preschool Enrollment Rates, 1870–1996

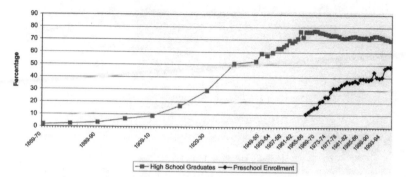

Note: The above figure is based on data from National Center for Education Statistics, *Digest of Education Statistics 1997*, Washington, D.C., table
6, p.15, http://nces.ed.gov/pubs/digest97to06.html (for preschool enrollment); National Center for Education Statistics, *Digest of Education Statistics 1997*, Washington, D.C., table 99, p.108, http://nces.ed.gov/pubs/
digest97to99.html.

domestic product (GDP) per capita than the public and private spending on early childhood education in all the afore-
mentioned countries, as well as in Canada, Denmark, Hungary, Sweden, Spain, Turkey, and the Netherlands.[32] State
and federal governments have provided so little funding to
preschools that it amounts to a parody of what is needed. For
example, Alabama spent $395 per poor child per year—even
including federal funding—or less than a dollar and a half
per day. California spent $536 per poor child—approxi-
mately half state funding and half federal funding—still
only about two dollars per day.[33] Given the cost of preschool, the lack of government funding means that many
families simply cannot afford to enroll their children.

We currently face grave problems of both quality and affordability. A 1998 study by the Consumer Product Safety Commission found safety hazards in two-thirds of licensed child care settings. The National Institute of Child Health and Development reported that 60 percent of preschool settings were poor or only fair in quality.[34] Moreover, although teachers of older children need certification, those caring for our youngest children are commonly not required to have either certification or any training in child development. While school districts have been trying to ensure smaller class sizes for older children, the majority of states still fail to meet the child-to-staff ratios for young children that are recommended by professional organizations, including the National Association for the Education of Young Children and the National Association of Child Care Resource and Referral Agencies.

Children under five are at critical developmental stages. So we should ensure that they are taught by teachers who are as well trained as teachers of elementary school children. We need to ensure that they are adequately paid, so that high-quality educators will continue to work in this area and so that the enormously high rates of staff turnover will decrease. Finally, we need to mandate adequate child-to-adult ratios. We should guarantee high-quality early education for all families, just as many European countries already do.[35] Only with public funding will low-income children have a shot at quality early education, which is essential to providing lower-income children with an equal opportunity for academic success.

Care for School-Age Children

We need to expand the opportunities for elementary and secondary school children as well. There is nothing magical about the current short school day and 180-day school year. Over the past 130 years, the length of the school year has been changed to meet the needs of families and children. As the amount of material children needed to learn in school for their economic survival increased, so too did the length of the school year. From 1870 to 1930, during a period of rapid industrialization, the length of the school year increased 30 percent, from 132 days to 173 days.[36] Then the expansion of public education stalled; from 1930 to the present, the school term has increased only seven days, from 173 days to 180 days.[37] Leaving the agrarian school calendar behind and extending educational opportunity are long overdue. These changes are important for both children and parents.

Few states have invested adequately in extending school programs, though considerable evidence argues for such extension. With the exception of Hawaii, in no state do more than half of all public schools have extended days. In more than half of the states, no more than one in five public schools offer after-school programs. Parental demand markedly outstrips supply nationwide. The federal government's efforts are currently focused on the Twenty-first Century Community Learning Centers initiative, which provides limited funding to communities so that they can provide services for children and families during after-school hours, including tutoring, mentoring, homework centers, academic enrichment activities, sports, and arts. The idea is very promising, but the centers touch only a fraction of the need.[38] For the more than 55 million school-age children in the United States, the funds amount to less than fifteen dollars per child per year—enough to pay for little more than one afternoon.[39] We ought to make access to academic extended-day and -year programs universal. When extended school and after-school programs are provided, they must be of high quality. The ability, training, and number of staff are all critical factors in the quality of programs. The relationships the programs have with the children's schools, families, and communities are equally crucial.

Extending educational opportunities for school-age children is important for working families, but the potential benefits go far beyond school. Many economists have argued that how individuals and families fare in a global economy increasingly depends on their educational attainment. Political scientists and policy makers agree that the welfare of communities and nations will depend on the educational attainment of their citizens. But in international mathematics achievement tests, scores for U.S. students in 1997 ranked behind, in order, those of students in Singapore, Japan, Korea, Hong Kong, Belgium, the Czech Republic, Austria, Hungary, the Slovak Republic, Switzerland, France, Slovenia, Bulgaria, the Netherlands, Canada, Ireland, Australia, Israel, Thailand, Sweden, Germany, New Zealand, Norway, and England. Furthermore, the eighth-grade science scores of U.S. students ranked behind those of students in twenty-one of the same countries tested.[40] Extending the school day and the school year would simultaneously provide more educational opportunities for children who need to be able to compete economically and help working parents who need their children to receive enrichment activities and quality supervision in a safe place. The use of existing school buildings would reduce the costs of these programs and increase their accessibility.

Not only is the U.S. educational system failing to measure up against that of other countries, but it currently fails to measure up against the fundamental American principle of equal opportunity. At present, children from affluent families typically spend their after-school hours and summer days in enrichment activities. Children from poor families too often spend those hours alone or in the inadequate care of other young children. Teachers commonly observe that over the course of the summer, the skills of marginalized children fall further behind as they forget some of what they have learned during the school-year—and in contrast, children who have had enrichment opportunities move ahead.

Providing a public opportunity for enrichment activities during the after-school hours and summer days would narrow the class disparities in how American children fare educationally.

Care for Elderly and Disabled Adults

Caring for families is about more than meeting the needs of children. Between 1870 and 1990, the U.S. population increased sixfold, but the population of Americans sixty-five years and older increased twenty-seven-fold.[41] Although those sixty-five years and older accounted for just over 1 million Americans (3 percent of the population) in 1870, as of 1999 there were over 34 million older Americans (13 percent of the population). By the year 2030, the U.S. Census Bureau estimates that there will be approximately 70 million Americans sixty-five and older (20 percent of the population).[42]

Although a great range of experience exists among older individuals, they are more likely than younger people to face limitations in their activities. Although fewer than one in twenty adults under sixty-five are limited in their ability to care for themselves, one in five adults sixty-five years or older has difficulty bathing, dressing, or getting around inside or outside the home.[43] Only a small minority of sixty- and seventy-year-olds have significant limitations, but the probability of having health problems increases with age.

We need to ensure that there are affordable solutions for meeting the daily as well as the urgent needs of the elderly.

Yet caring for the elderly will in some ways present far greater challenges than caring for children. When we consider how to expand educational opportunities for school-age children, we are considering a 25 percent increase in the school day or the school year—an increase that is likely to have a clear long-run economic return, which will offset some of the costs. Meeting the long-range needs of the elderly at first glance appears to be an overwhelming task. But it is not as daunting as it first seems. Moreover, as society focuses on other needs, those of the elderly are growing, not going away.

Clear steps can be taken both to decrease the need for long-term care and to improve the quality of life for older Americans. We must eliminate age discrimination in the workplace, so that older Americans who want to work can do so. We must ensure that the Americans with Disabilities Act is successfully implemented and enforced, so that the same is true for disabled Americans. Not only is income from work important to self-sufficiency, but intellectual and physical stimulation have repeatedly been demonstrated to play a critical role in health, longevity, and minimizing disability.

We should ensure that the elderly and disabled Americans who are not working have sufficient opportunities for exercise, social interaction, and intellectual stimulation— all essential ingredients for their ability to live as healthy and independent lives as possible.[44] When these opportunities include volunteer work, the elderly and disabled will be able to contribute to communities at the same time. We must ensure that those who cannot live alone without support but are not in need of twenty-four-hour care get the amount of help necessary for them to continue to live at home and avoid the far greater social, personal, and economic costs of being unnecessarily institutionalized.

The critical question of long-term care insurance—how to pay for the care of those who need twenty-four-hour nursing home or other care—will remain. But both the need for and cost of that care will be reduced if we provide elderly and disabled adults with sufficient opportunities and supports for continuing to live independently, and if we provide their family members with the necessary leave from work to help when urgent needs arise.

Affordable and Necessary

Other nations have demonstrated the economic viability of providing basic family benefits. Countries with a wide range of economic, political, and social structures have demonstrated the feasibility of paid maternity leave. From Germany to Gabon, from Belgium to Brazil, from Switzerland to Senegal, women receive paid maternity leave.[45] Providing paid paternity leave is no less affordable. Access to early childhood education is ensured in Denmark, Finland, Sweden, France, Belgium, Italy, Germany, and Britain.[46]

When it comes to school-age children, the United States is far from the top in spending on education. Public spending on education, as a percentage of GDP per capita, is higher in Austria, Canada, Denmark, Finland, France, Iceland, Luxembourg, New Zealand, Norway, Poland, Portugal, Sweden, and Switzerland.[47] What's more, in contrast to our 180-day average, the school year is 220 days in the Netherlands, Luxembourg, and Italy; in Germany, 213 days.[48]

What will making the needed changes on a national level mean to employers? On balance, the changes will make it easier for employers to get their essential work done well. Employees who currently must miss work because they cannot find child care for preschool or school-age children will not need to do so when we have quality early education and extended school days available nationwide. Employees who have had to miss work to register a child for school or their families for food stamps will not need to do so when public services either increase their hours or expand their registration and reenrollment methods to include mail, phone, fax, or the Internet. Employees who now must take off an hour and a half every day to transport a child to an after-school program will no longer need to leave work for this purpose when adequate transportation services are developed. Although in some cases necessary absences may increase—such as when parents use their newly available leave time to be with sick children who should not be left at home alone—these will be balanced by the drop in preventable absences. Whereas now companies that offer good conditions for working families have to compete with companies that offer none, universal benefits will level the playing field nationally.

Addressing the needs of working families will no more

threaten our economy than providing public education or ensuring basic safety standards for workers has. In fact, many of the essential steps will strengthen our economy, just as providing public education has done. In the long run, our international competitiveness is determined by the quality of our labor force. Both by making it possible for all Americans—irrespective of income, gender, or caretaking responsibilities—to contribute in the workplace to their full potential, and by improving the educational opportunities and support available to children who will join the labor force in a generation, these reforms will strengthen our ability to compete.

We can afford to make the needed changes; we cannot afford to continue our current practices. Making changes on a national scale is necessary if all American working families are to have a chance. Perhaps most overlooked in the entire debate about addressing the needs of working families is how fundamental this effort is to equal opportunity in our country. If we do not take the needs of working families as a keystone, the gaps between the prospects of poor, middle-class, and rich children will only grow wider.

As a nation we face critical choices. Will poor working parents and their children continue to face far worse odds than other families? What will happen to a sizable fraction of the middle class—particularly those families in which a child or adult has special needs? Will they all be left behind? Or will we bring our social institutions into the twenty-first century?

Much of what must be done extends past reforms. In the past, we have expanded public education for high school; expanding early education is equally important now. We have school days and calendars that matched the agrarian work cycle; we should update them to match parents' industrial and postindustrial work schedule and children's increasing need for high-level skills. We have Social Security that responds to the income needs of older Americans; we must respond to their other needs as well. We have national unemployment insurance that dates from a time when the loss of the single wage earner's job was the largest threat; we need paid family leave insurance for the current workforce, for whom loss of work is as likely to result from the need of an adult to be home to provide care for a family member. We have adequate transportation systems for healthy adults, we should have equally good ones to link children and adults in need to their caregivers. Ultimately, all that is required is the depth of commitment borne of the recognition that our nation's future depends on effective action.

2

FREEDOM AND OPPORTUNITY

JEAN BETHKE ELSHTAIN

Let's begin with two claims about American political culture. First, the United States is defined primarily as the "land of liberty." Our current war against terrorism of global reach is named "Operation Enduring Freedom," not "Operation Equal Opportunity" or something similar, and this for good reason. Freedom is the great and abiding American standard. An anthem of the antislavery movement was the great slave song "Oh Freedom," a hymn at once lament and dream, and it went like this: "Oh Freedom, Oh Freedom / Oh Freedom over me / And before I'd be a slave / I'd be buried in my grave / And go home to my Lord and be free." Second, one dimension of American freedom in the minds and dreams of those born here and those who came, and come, here is opportunity. That was certainly the case for my own immigrant grandparents. The United States was the land where human beings, by the sweat of their brow, could make a living, maybe own a piece of land. The opportunity was there. The costs were huge, and in our case included backbreaking labor as hired sugar beet harvesters from dawn to dusk in the baking sun of northern Colorado's high plains. This labor included children. As a result, the two oldest children in my grandparents' family—my own mother and one of my aunts—were compelled to quit school after eighth grade in order to labor in the fields. Within a few years, the necessity for that regime altered sufficiently so that my mother's other three siblings were able to complete high school. But all sixteen of my grandparents' grandchildren had a college education of one sort of another, with a few of us going on for higher degrees.

In many ways this is the typical American immigrant story. And because it is, pushing a version of equality that goes much beyond the theme of opportunity and hard work is difficult to sell in our political culture. Too many Americans have made it into the middle class and have made it in what might be called the old-fashioned way. But what was the old-fashioned way? What did we have that enabled so many of us, who do not come from privilege, to keep working hard and to realize at least some of our own—and our society's—vision of the American dream? We had strong families with what now is called a "stay-at-home" mother, although that doesn't begin to capture what women did in these communities. For women were a mainstay of American civil society, nurturing and sustaining many of the communal and civic institutions that eased and blurred the edges of economic difference. And we had strong, competent teachers—all women until high school—in the local school that housed grades one through twelve in a single building: our village had only 185 people, after all. Single women who had never married, or quit teaching when they did, and married women whose own children had grown dominated the teaching profession. The result was that in this little place my own training in "the basics" was extraordinary.

That was essentially it. We felt the hand of government, when I was growing up, in foreign policy mostly—it was the era of the Cold War. We recognized it in our public schools, but they were under local control, and local tax levies primarily funded them, so government's role was minimal. We recognized it in the huge interstate highway system developed by the Eisenhower administration. We recognized it in Social Security and other provisions made for those who were incapacitated by an accident at work or some other catastrophe and needed a temporary—for that is how we thought of it—hand up. We knew that veterans received housing assistance and had special hospitals, and I learned when I started college just how many of my professors were veterans who, not being people of privilege themselves, had attained their college education via the GI Bill.

All of this fit with the dominating ethos of our political culture, a point made ably a few years back by distinguished political sociologist Theda Skocpol in her book *Protecting Soldiers and Mothers*. She demonstrates what Jody Heymann fails to recognize and seems unaware of, namely, that the American form of social provision goes back at least to the Civil War era and the task of tending, as our greatest president put it, to the "widows and orphans" and to those who "should have borne the battle." Assistance was tied to honored and necessary tasks—soldiering and mothering.

These tasks were, of course, gender-specific in that era. But the more salient point for our era is that all of this made good political sense and did not stir widespread resentment at perceived unfairness. Doing the task one is called upon to do sometimes deserves benefits unavailable to those who do not undertake such tasks. Few would cavil at that.

But many cavil at going much further than that, or presumably we would have in place a much more extensive social provision and assistance system than in fact we do. These are legislative matters, after all, and legislators are elected. When many of the working-class people who are hypothetically supposed to be at the receiving end of certain dramatic alterations in how we tax and spend oppose those changes, what is one to do: push even harder for them or rethink one's strategy?

How does this apply to Heymann's hypothesized social democracy, modeled very much on standards in the European social democracies that are now in trouble or have altered the way they do business by moving away from the sorts of policies Heymann proposes? These social democracies—Norway and Sweden come to mind—are in trouble, not because a cadre of determined libertarians set out to destroy a vast array of social provisions and public goods, but because they are internally less and less sustainable given a declining tax base. As I read Heymann's essay, a refrain kept echoing: How is this to be funded? European social democracies are in trouble in part because the birth rate is below the replacement level in many countries and because the population is aging and living longer. That means stretching tax dollars—or Euros now—to sustain people much beyond what were average life spans when many of these regimes moved to a strong social welfare state—from cradle to grave, as the saying goes.

The implications are rather stark and simple: you are never going to push through forms of social provision and assistance in the United States unless you can demonstrate (a) that the proposed new policies are affordable and sustainable and (b) that the proposed new policies are consistent with the basic themes of American political culture that honors equality of opportunity and an honest reward—fair recompense—for hard work. I am not saying that Heymann cannot make this case. I am saying that she has not. A major problem is that she simply hasn't defined many of her basic terms. She speaks of the absorption of women in the labor force—as but one example—with the result that "more than 70 percent of children live in households in which every parent was in the labor force." But this doesn't sufficiently disaggregate—as social scientists like to say—the data. How many of these parents are single parents—a defining factor in how children fare? How many parents, especially mothers, work full time? This, too, bears on outcomes for children in a significant way. The devil is in the details, and we get too few details. It is one thing for government to play a role in caring for American children. It is another for government to become the nurturer of first resort, so to speak, and that is the direction of a good bit of

Heymann's argument. I say "appears" because she needs to do a lot more to unpack her underlying rationale. It seems that she finds the family one of those "outdated social institutions." As she well knows, you don't make that assumption and get very far in our political culture. There are ways that Heymann could retool her argument to make it more consistent with the basic values that animate our political culture. The point that too many of our children are falling through the net of equal opportunity, through no fault of their own, is one of these. But in privileging economic factors and forces, as Heymann has done, and ignoring, for the most part, cultural and historical forces, which she has also done, her argument is going to die aborning once it hits the light of political day. If I were Heymann, I would argue that our political culture relies heavily on the presupposition that somehow we are all in it together—a point the attacks of September 11, 2001, brought home in the most shocking way. And because we are all in it together, we cannot tolerate, over the long haul, fundamental and growing gaps in the ways of life that Americans lead and presume that the civic glue will hold. Is it the case that such a gap is growing? Heymann says yes. But she needs to do more to make that case and to explain *politically* why everything that she proposes is so exigent.

LIMITED OPTIONS

ANNE ALSTOTT

There is much to admire in Jody Heymann's essay. She deftly reveals the outmoded assumptions that shape American social policy. She offers practical programs that could improve the lives of vulnerable people—poor children and their parents. Heymann's work is a welcome effort to transcend these libertarian times and to harness the redistributive power of the state to the service of social justice.

Still, I have serious reservations about the limited conception of equality that may be suggested by Heymann's proposals. Heymann begins by invoking a broad, liberal-egalitarian principle of equal opportunity to motivate her program.[1] And her prescriptions for children would advance that goal, although more might be done. When it comes to adults, Heymann focuses specifically on mitigating the harsh working conditions that pit paid-work success against children's needs. But the equal opportunity principle—the idea that there should be "equal chances to succeed"—demands consideration for the aspirations of poor parents as *individuals* and not merely as *workers*. Thus the proposals Heymann presents here do not address the needs of poor parents who cannot or do not hold paid jobs. More fundamentally, job leave and day care programs, for example, fail to challenge the deeper injustices that limit the life options available to parents and to the poor: the choices they make about whether to enter the labor market or not in the first place. A better approach would focus in the first instance on expanding poor parents' options for combining paid work with child rearing and other life projects over time, not just on mitigating their burdens once they have taken on paid employment.

I want to emphasize that I am not simply urging that *more* be done for nonworking families; my disagreement with Heymann is not that her program is partial rather than comprehensive. I am suggesting, instead, that policies to ensure justice *for the working poor themselves* will look very different once we see that our basic aim is to ensure equal opportunity for *individuals* with limited resources, working or not. Though I think that the United States would be a more just country if we adopted Heymann's proposals, my conclusion is not that we need to supplement her proposals, but that we should explore a different design of basic policies.

Providing equal opportunity means offering all individuals the freedom to shape a life plan of their own choosing, regardless of class background, gender, or race. To this end, the state should commit adequate resources to the education and development of each child. All children deserve a chance to make meaningful choices among the different lives they might lead. Heymann's proposals for children proceed in this spirit. Public subsidies for preschool for poor children are an especially good idea, although universal public preschool, from age three through kindergarten, might be even better.[2] Realization of her proposals would represent substantial progress toward equal opportunity for children, though we also need to address the glaring inequalities in public education.

But a just society should also pay attention to opportunities for adults. Parents and the poor confront serious constraints on their capacity to choose and pursue different life plans. Parents care for their children for the long term, and they usually put children's needs ahead of their other life projects when circumstances demand it.[3] Poor people face obvious financial obstacles to life planning. And many poor adults were denied adequate educational and developmental resources as children. A liberal state should respond by enhancing the quality and range of life options that poor parents and individuals might pursue.

Today's families choose a variety of arrangements for combining paid work and child rearing. Although Heymann emphasizes mothers' increasing participation in the labor force, that trend is only part of a more complex picture. In 2000, for example, a slight majority (54 percent) of mothers worked full time, whereas 27 percent were not in the labor force at all, and another 16 percent worked part time.[4] This diversity persists throughout the income spectrum. Many families of modest means make economic sacrifices in order to care for their children themselves. For example, families with yearly incomes under $25,000 are at least as likely as more affluent families to have a mother who stays at home or works part time. The very poorest families have the most tenuous connection to paid work.[5] For them, job leave and day care policies offer highly uneven coverage, improving life for full-time workers but offering little to families with a disabled or unemployed worker or a mother whose child care responsibilities lead her to work part time or not at all.

Liberal equality counsels respect for parents' choices. Some parents work full time, for financial security and for the dignity they find in that endeavor. Others forgo income and job prospects to take time away from paid work to rear their children. For reasons of religion, tradition, or personal conviction, they believe that parental care is best.[6] Some have children with special needs, who require more intensive care than even a flexible paid job will permit. And these choices may change over time, as a family's needs and opportunities evolve.

Child rearing is not a mechanical task. It is value-laden work. For parents of all incomes, choices about child rearing express heartfelt purposes and aspirations. No matter how high the quality of day care or after-school programs, some families will strive to arrange their lives so that one—or both—parents can provide personal care. These facts indicate some important limits on the role of day care and paid job leave in advancing equal opportunity. To be sure, some parents might gladly seize the opportunities to work that Heymann's programs would extend. But it is also essential to support parents' ability to choose among a variety of options.

For example, public policy should recognize that children's emergencies can disrupt family life, whether or not each parent holds a full-time job. The problem of *work* disruption is really a special case of *life* disruption. A child with a serious illness, a developmental disability, or an educational crisis will require large investments of parental time and energy, interfering with family work at home as well as performance on the job. Instead of paid job leave just for workers, or a conjunction of paid job leave for workers with support focused on nonworking families, we might consider an encompassing program of "crisis insurance" for families, which would provide appropriate support, including financial help but also home help and social work resources, to every affected household.[7]

In a similar vein, public policy should endeavor to expand *child care* options rather than *day care* programs. Universal preschool is a sound proposal for ensuring that every child comes to kindergarten ready for school. But extended-day programs and other day care subsidies should not be the exclusive source of support for child care outside the standard school day. Full-time workers bear the obvious financial costs of day care, but parents who care for children at home incur opportunity costs, measured not only in lost wages but also in lost "human capital" and retirement contributions. A more encompassing program might offer each family an annual grant, which could be used to purchase child care, to pay for a parent's education or training when reentering the workforce, or to contribute to a retirement plan. It is not difficult to imagine a cafeteria-style program that would offer every family a menu of options.

Heymann argues that after-school programs and longer school years could improve children's educational outcomes. If these programs are the best way to redress inequalities in education, they deserve serious consideration. But emphasizing education—rather than day care—raises new questions. For example, resources might be better spent on more intensive academic programs (e.g., tutoring) directed to students who need extra academic support. However long the educationally sound school day or year, children will still need residual care, and parents should have a range of options for providing it. This is particularly true for infants and toddlers under age three, who would not be eligible for preschool.

Heymann's focus on crafting policies targeted specifically at poor *working* parents may reflect the conventional assumption that poor parents have no choice—they must work. It is true that poor families struggle to make ends meet in low-wage jobs. But the financial constraint itself is an artifact of public policy, not a law of nature. Labor markets may allocate resources efficiently, but they cannot distribute to every individual the resources needed to make meaningful choices among life options. Paid job leave, transportation help, and after-school programs could ameliorate working conditions for poor workers. But equal opportunity supports a broad effort to underwrite the educational, social, and financial resources necessary for poor people to engage in life planning. Stakeholding or basic income, for example, could alleviate the financial constraint with an unconditional cash grant for all individuals. Additional programs should address the educational and social injustices that contribute to poverty. Adult education and training are worth discussing, as are geographic-mobility programs, which offer poor people the chance to leave blighted areas for more stable neighborhoods offering the "social capital" that supports wider opportunities.

All these proposals are controversial, and every one requires more sustained justification and explication than this short essay can provide.[8] My intention here is merely to suggest the generative potential of a broader vision of equal opportunity. True equality would endow individuals with resources to form a vision of the good life and to pursue that vision. Tolerance and mutual respect are most familiar in debates over free speech, where the First Amendment protects the expression of diverse ideas. The same values should inform our social policy. In a just society, people should have a chance not only to talk about diverse ideals but to live them.

THE VALUE OF CARE

JOAN TRONTO

Feminists have argued for years that care needs to be more valued, and Jody Heymann's argument is a welcome addition to this debate.[1] Yet there are limits to starting from liberal principles of justice and equality and expecting the value of care simply to fit within that framework. Heymann's argument—that equality of opportunity demands that family time for caring should be equalized—represents such an approach. Heymann argues that if time were organized more rationally around care, then more children would have better chances of success in school, more elderly relatives would receive adequate attention, work and productivity would improve, and society would be the better for it.[2]

There is a basic flaw in this argument: as long as caring remains a subordinate activity and value within the framework of a competitive, "winner-take-all" society, caring well within one's family will make one not a friend but an enemy of equal opportunity. In order to see this flaw, let us work from the personal to the social level and then consider an alternative.

Because we do not typically think of care in any terms except the intimate and personal, we usually translate this value into the preexisting models of family caregiving. When we care, we do not think of society, we think of our intimates and their concrete and particular needs. In a competitive society, what it means to care well for one's own children is to make sure that they have a competitive edge against other children. On the most concrete level, although parents may endorse a principle of equality of opportunity in the abstract, their daily activities are most visibly "caring" when they gain special privileges and advantages for their children. Arguments about the value of universal public education and so forth lose their force when they affect the possibility of *our* children's future. This example demonstrates that when care is embedded in another framework of values, it does not necessarily lead in a progressive direction.

Let us move the analysis from an individual to a social level. Valuable though care is, one way to understand a group's social power is in seeing whether it is able to force some other people to carry out its caregiving work. The distribution of care work thus reflects power. It is not simply a matter of irrational tradition that has shaped the transformation of work and care from agrarian to industrial to postindustrial schedules. The privatization of reproductive care that has accompanied the increasingly public nature of productive work reflects as well the relative social power of different groups to make their contributions more highly prized and recognized. Relatively more powerful people in society have a lot at stake in seeing that their caring needs are met under conditions that are beneficial to them, even if this means that the caring needs of those who provide them with services are neglected. More powerful people can fob off caregiving work on to others: men to women, upper to lower class, free men to slaves. Care work itself is often demanding and inflexible, and not all of it is productive. People who do such work recognize its intrinsic value, but it does not fit well in a society that values innovation and accumulation of wealth.

Idealized middle-class family care in the United States thus requires, structures, and perpetuates some of the very inequities of care that Heymann describes. A "career person" wants only what is best for his or her family.[3] This leads to the assumption that such people care for themselves and that "care" is a concern only for the dependent and infirm —that is, the young, the unhealthy, and the old. In fact, the model of the self-caring breadwinner is a deception: although working adults may not require the expert assistance of professional caregivers, they may use a great deal of other people's *care services* (that is, routine caring work) to keep their busy lives on keel.[4] In American society, the more elite one becomes, the more dependent one becomes upon others to satisfy one's basic caring needs: edible food, clean clothing, functional, attractive shelter. Thus the parents who have flexible work schedules and whose children succeed at school are probably using a vast array of care services. Such labor is among the poorest paid and least well organized in our society. Heymann's widening gap is thus also a caregiving gap, though the ideology of private family "caring" covers up its roots and makes it more intractable.

{ 52 }

There can be no doubt that what Jody Heymann has demonstrated is that among the other problems and burdens they face, the less well off in our society also have fewer resources at their disposal to meet their caregiving needs. In the long run, the only way to remedy this situation is to recognize a universal need for care. Care is not the concern only of the young, old, and infirm. Everyone needs and uses care, just as everyone provides care. One of the reasons in our society that people struggle so hard to make more money is to provide more of what they think of as these necessities to their families. Change can occur only if we radically imagine a societal structure that no longer requires that people compete against each other to make sure that their basic needs will be adequately met. Such a society will conceive of care not as a private good but as a broad and public value.

THE PLACE OF EDUCATION

JAMES P. COMER

Jody Heymann addresses a challenge facing the United States that is as important as "Homeland Security" but is less apparent and draws much less attention. The more subtle nature of the problem certainly makes it as dangerous. As she points out, the fabric and future of American society is threatened by the prospect that a growing number of Americans are not able to experience the American Dream.

The belief that if one works hard and plays by the rules one will have a reasonable chance of succeeding as a child and an adult (the American Dream) is a central organizing and motivating force in our society. This, and a growing respect for founding ideals and the rule of law, has moved our society from acts of genocide and slavery, as well as the oppression of immigrants, women, and children, to the point of becoming the most powerful force for humane living in the world, perhaps in the history of the world. But changes in the nature of the economy have weakened the family in a way that makes it difficult for too many to rear their children well. If we do not reverse these tendencies, our quality of life will decline—slowly at first, and then precipitously, as many more in generation after generation are excluded from the dream.[1]

Throughout human history, children have grown up in close proximity to their families and a primary social network of friends, kin, and communal organizations (the village) in which they felt a sense of belonging. Children and parents were able to form powerful emotional attachments and bonds.[2] Living conditions were often poor, but one head of family, without an education, could usually provide a reasonable living for his or her dependents, and the other could usually provide home and community support for child and youth development.

Children were able to identify with, imitate, and internalize the attitudes, values, and ways of their parents and other members of their network. The adults in the network were able to help them grow along the critical developmental pathways (sociointeractive, psychoemotional, ethical, linguistic, cognitive-intellectual). In these powerful relationship settings, most children were able to establish habits, beliefs, and behaviors that enabled them to become successful as youngsters and as adults, and this promoted desirable social functioning.

But the relentless, 150-year march from an agricultural economy through an industrial to a science- and technology-based economy has not only pulled both parents into the workforce but also removed "the village" that once helped parents rear their children.[3] Despite the speed and magnitude of this change, the needs of children remain the same as they were in antiquity—children require protection and support for development. Importantly, they now need a higher level of development in order to get the level of education required to be able to function well in this complex age. The sad fact, however, is that the developmental support many currently receive would be inadequate in any society.

Because of modern communication technologies, children receive an enormous amount of information. For the first time in the history of the world, information goes directly to children without a chance for censor or censure on the part of responsible adults. There are too few people available to help young people examine the information and to encourage an appropriate response. Because of high mobility, many of the adults in their lives—teachers, police, doctors, and other service providers—are essentially strangers. And again, often the only parent or both parents are in the workforce and busy. All of this creates burdensome and disorganizing levels of stress, which is a major cause of divorce and the creation of single-parent families. For these and other reasons, many parents are not able to provide their families with the quality and level of care necessary for adequate development today.

Our society has been slow to recognize the effects of change and the range of services needed to reduce the stress on families and to make it possible for them to rear their children well in today's world. Instead, we blame families for not adequately performing their child rearing tasks. Family and child advocates call for more and better child care options for working parents and better education for children. Both are very much needed but are not sufficient. Moreover, traditional education cannot do the job of parenting. And fragmented social services, without a context of meaningful relationships, can't provide children with the experiences that will enable them to become successful as youngsters and as adults.

Traditional education has put the cart before the horse. It focuses on curriculum, instruction, assessment, and technology first, and child and youth development second, if at all. Many of our school problems stem from the fact that many of our children are underdeveloped and therefore unprepared for academic learning. Most school staff are not prepared to help them grow. This leads to staff and student underachievement and failure. Generally, school systems have not taken responsibility for the earliest years of childhood, now shown to be very important in providing the platform for later learning.

Nonetheless, the school is the only institution in our society positioned to reduce family stress and to provide the essential elements of the traditional "village." All children go to school. The mission is highly positive. There are more adults available in schools who can offer children positive growth-producing interaction than anywhere else. Also, the school can provide a context in which other service providers—health, recreation, and community organizations (arts, athletics, other opportunities for positive self-expression)—can engage with young people in a coordinated, purposeful, and sustained way.

Brought together to support social development and maturity, the programs of a range of service providers could be designed to help students acquire the critical capacities once provided almost exclusively in family networks. But to do so, our education system needs a perspective oriented to child and youth development from birth through sixteen years of schooling. This will require changes in the theory and practice of public education, in graduate schools of education, and among policy and opinion makers. All must understand how to put the horse before the cart: development before curriculum, instruction, assessment, and technology. When educators take on the role of helping young people grow and function rather than merely trying to transmit information, student resistance and struggle will diminish.

In 1968, our Yale Child Study Center School Development Program (SDP) went into two inner-city elementary schools in New Haven. The students were almost all black and from families under severe economic and social stress. They were thirty-second and thirty-third in academic achievement and had the worst attendance and behavior in the city. By applying the principles of the behavioral and social sciences to every aspect of the school program, we helped parents and staff recreate "the village" in school in a way that actively encouraged student development. Good teaching and learning became possible. The students eventually achieved the third- and fourth-highest ranks in academic achievement (putting the school on par with those in wealthier neighborhoods), and they produced the best attendance record in the city, with no serious behavior problems.[4]

This approach is still being replicated, and where the implementation is sound, the outcomes are good. In 2000, a similar school in Detroit, using the SDP focus on development, achieved the highest scores in Michigan on statewide tests for fourth graders.[5] But the experiences they received that helped them grow and prepared them for life are probably more important. We are now working with school districts, schools of education, policy and opinion leaders. It is our hope that these efforts will ignite a national movement to put the focus in schools on development and thus prepare students for the challenges of modern life.

In short, rapid scientific and technological change weakened the vital infrastructure for development, teaching and learning, and preparation for life. But with policies and programs geared to restore the essential elements of this infrastructure, we may be able to recreate the social fabric of the "village," and offer a generation of children a real chance at realizing the American dream.

THE POLITICAL BIND

THEDA SKOCPOL

Socioeconomic inequalities have grown to an alarming extent in the United States over the past generation. The gap is especially sharp between privileged families headed by two higher-educated, fully employed professionals and all other families. For Americans without advanced degrees or inherited wealth, the new reality is stark: even if men and women manage to marry and stay together, wages and benefits once earned by one breadwinner-provider now must be earned by two parents holding down two or three jobs. Time to care for children and other family members often gets squeezed out.

Several factors have converged to propel inequality—including premium wages for people with advanced education or technical skills, intensified economic competition in an era of globalization, and the drastic decline of blue-collar unions. But the failure of U.S. social provision is also a prime culprit. High earners enjoy tax-subsidized employee benefits, and they can fill any gaps by purchasing quality child care, elder care, and enhanced pensions or health services on the private market. But Americans who earn modest or poverty-level wages are stuck. Their employers may not offer pensions or health insurance at all, and few of them can take paid time off to care for sick children or disabled relatives, or to attend school conferences.

To make matters much worse, U.S. public social programs also fail working families of modest means. Medicare and Medicaid do not reach the more than 40 million Americans now without health insurance, most of whom are in low-wage working families. U.S. Family and Medical Leave legislation provides no compensation for lost wages and does not cover employees of small businesses. And our nation does little to fund high-quality child care, after-school programs, or long-term care for the elderly. Public programs in most advanced industrial democracies find ways to correct for the inequities and failures of the private wage market, but U.S. programs (apart from Social Security) exacerbate market disparities. Inequality thus becomes ever more entrenched, as the children of less privileged parents find themselves ill prepared to compete for the best jobs of the future.

New public supports for working families could correct this alarming situation, Jody Heymann suggests. She bases her case in part on a principle of equal opportunity, but then she also suggests, in rationalist language reminiscent of appeals made by early-twentieth-century Progressive reformers, that U.S. economic efficiency would be enhanced by strong family supports: "addressing the needs of working families," she says, "will strengthen our ability to compete." She suggests that "other nations have demonstrated the economic viability of providing basic family benefits," and such provision will "on balance . . . make it easier for employers to get their essential work done well." While emphasizing these economic benefits, Heymann underplays the costs of a new family policy: she asserts that "we can afford to make the needed changes," but she never indicates what the overall cost might be. She concludes by suggesting that in completing the construction of our very partial system of social provision, "ultimately, all that is required is the depth of commitment borne of the recognition that our nation's future depends on effective action."

Much as I admire and agree with Heymann's policy analysis, I am troubled by the absence of any attention to the cultural-political opposition that her proposals will provoke. Her concluding account of costs and benefits strikes me as politically naive, for it fails to take into account fierce opposition from conservatives, who proclaim that individuals and families should "take responsibility" for themselves and make their own way in unfettered markets. American social programs are not just out of adjustment with changing family patterns. They are caught in the vortex of a sharp rightward shift in national politics.

From the mid-nineteenth through the mid-twentieth century, generous and relatively inclusive social programs were enacted and expanded in U.S. democracy. The United States never built a European-style welfare state focused on wage earners, but it did spread public education, create extraordinarily generous benefits for the veterans of the Civil War and World War II, enact national and state-level pro-

grams to assist mothers and children, and establish the Social Security system, later enhanced by Medicare, to protect
elderly retirees. In all of these cases, public programs were
devised to benefit middle-class as well as less-privileged
Americans—and the programs were widely understood,
not as "welfare" for the poor, but as protections or opportunities open to many Americans who contribute to the nation
and deserve public benefits in return. From women's groups
and veterans' associations to unions and movements of the
elderly, massive voluntary associations were involved in agi-
tating for new social legislation, and then they teamed up
with government to implement social programs. Politically
successful social programs were able to sustain broad popular support across class lines and had access to secure and rising sources of tax revenue.

In my recent work, I analyze the politics that lay behind
major U.S. social programs in the past, and I show that from
the 1960s onward, possibilities for enacting additional inclusive social programs broke down.[1] After the civil rights
struggles, liberals turned to poverty programs and affir-
mative action regulations, while conservatives orchestrated
popular backlashes against the use of public tax revenues to
pay for "welfare" programs targeted only at some very poor
people. Working- and middle-class Americans, especially
whites, came to resent public expenditures on health care
and education programs for which their families were not
eligible. A more universal program, Social Security, re-
mained much more popular. But starting in the 1980s, con-

servatives orchestrated attacks on Social Security too, trying to persuade younger middle-class Americans that the public system is too expensive to sustain and that they can get a better deal if their taxes are used to establish individualized market accounts on Wall Street. Heymann takes the continuing existence of Social Security for granted and wants to build on it. But Social Security itself is now under attack.

In our time, conservative Republicans and Democrats have delegitimated the very notion of nationally managed social provision, while enacting repeated tax cuts that starve the federal government of the future revenues it will need for Social Security and Medicare—let alone the resources to fund adequate universal family supports of the sort advocated by Heymann. Even now, as Americans experience a rush of patriotism, national solidarity, and renewed faith in government amid our new war against international terrorism, conservatives continue to push for tax cuts. At best, trade unionists, liberal Democrats, and other progressives fight rearguard actions to preserve surviving social programs.

The playing field is tilted, because political parties and voluntary associations no longer reach out to activate and inform masses of ordinary Americans. Moneyed interests and professionally run advocacy groups dominate the political process. Few alternative voices gain access to the media—which profoundly influence the attitudes of the public, measured in turn by pollsters who tell elected politicians what can and cannot be done. In this situation it is much easier to sell distrust of government and tax cuts than to build broad majority support for any expensive new social program. Here is the political bind faced by those who want enhanced social provision: in the United States public assistance to the poor is politically sustainable only when channeled through broad public programs that also include the middle class. But universal programs are expensive—hard to launch or sustain in a time of dwindling public revenues.

In this new American political context—as the rich not only get richer but are able to manipulate the public agenda and hobble democratic government in the interests of the majority—Heymann's reasonable arguments may very well fall on deaf ears. The cycle of ever-exacerbated inequality she portrays will not be interrupted by cost-benefit appeals alone. Instead, working men and women—assembled in popularly rooted institutions such as churches, trade unions, and translocally linked community groups—will have to find a way to forge a new majority movement, calling for family protections for all Americans. Heymann's vision of security and opportunity for all can help to inform and inspire such a movement. But it will take more than reasonable argument to get there.

ADDING GENDER AND WORK

LOTTE BAILYN

Jody Heymann paints a disturbing picture of what is happening to our nation's children, particularly those of the less affluent, and the consequences of this for the future of our society. In a well-documented essay, she alerts us to the need for national policies that seem almost obvious and are clearly economically feasible, since countries with much weaker economies than ours have found it possible to support them. But given the present economic situation and the underlying philosophy of the current administration, the chance that any of these sensible and achievable ideas will be implemented is remote at best.

Heymann's portrait of the disconnect between current national and employment policies on the one hand and the caregiving needs of contemporary families on the other constitutes a damning statement about our national priorities. And by complementing other efforts that discuss this lack of connection (e.g., Mona Harrington's *Care and Equality*, Joan Williams's *Unbending Gender*, and the Report of the Sloan Work-Family Policy Network), it contributes to a growing body of knowledge about the current crisis of care in the United States, particularly with regard to the care of children, but also care of the elderly, of working adults themselves, and of the community at large.[1]

Though there are many points of similarity among these analyses, and even an emerging consensus on many of the necessary reforms, Heymann's otherwise convincing and important statement omits discussion of two crucial points that are necessary for a full understanding of the situation. One concerns the role of gender and the other concerns the design of work itself.

Both Harrington and Williams consider gender critical because the social practices and ideologies that are the prime contributors to the problem they and Heymann so vividly portray are constructed around it. Harrington calls for a new understanding of family, one that does not separate a public masculine world of paid employment from a private feminine domain of care. New government or employer policies based on a traditional view of family, she fears, will only further reinforce existing inequities between men and women. Williams's analysis shows that the traditional masculine definition of an ideal worker—as someone whose sole responsibility and engagement is with paid work—is discriminatory under current law toward anyone (usually women) with caretaking responsibilities. As such, she suggests a legal strategy to deal with these issues. Bringing the lens of gender to the discussion, therefore, can warn us of important social consequences and alert us to new policy alternatives.[2]

Missing also is a detailed look at the organization of work and the role that work practices as currently defined play in the crisis of care. Heymann rightly points to the need for workplace flexibility. But, though flexibility can clearly be useful, if it is superimposed on current ways of structuring work, it cannot achieve the dual imperatives of caretaking and gender equity. What is needed is a deeper cultural change that would legitimate the needs of family care both in the design of work and in the assumptions about competence and success that surround it. Also needed is a new definition of an ideal worker, who, by integrating paid work with family care, better meets both productivity and caring needs.

For example, Heymann suggests extending the availability of social services beyond the nine-to-five workday. But what happens to the families of the employees who have to staff these extended hours? For them, the work-family dilemma gets exacerbated. The alternative of changing workplace practices that demand a worker's continuous eight-hour presence and giving all employees a few "working" hours a week to attend to such needs is not considered, because we assume that then productivity would suffer. But there is plenty of evidence, from both experimental and action research, that the extra motivation generated by such legitimation would lead to at least as much productive work as before, if not more. It is only the assumption that work as currently organized cannot be changed without harm that stands in the way. My colleagues and I have been collaborating with organizations for some time to test the hypothesis that it is possible to make changes in work design that help employees with their personal needs while at the same time enhancing the business goals of the organization. The results, chronicled in our new book, indicate that despite the difficulty of challenging workplace assumptions, structural change that benefits all is possible. [3]

Finally, change also needs to take place in the family. And here the efforts of the Third Path Institute in Philadelphia are important. Under Jessica DeGroot's leadership, the institute is working with couples and with family and career counselors to build cultural and structural conditions that honor collaborative, equitable patterns of caring and earning.

I am in complete agreement with Heymann's conclusion that "by making it possible for all Americans—irrespective of income, gender, or caretaking responsibilities—to contribute in the workplace to their full potential, and by improving the educational opportunities and support available to children who will join the labor force in a generation, these reforms will strengthen our ability to compete." But to convince a society ideologically committed to the separation of the public sphere of economic work from the private domestic arena of care, with the latter a matter only of individual choice, we will need a better understanding of the way our social patterns are gendered as well as the way these affect the assumptions on which our workplace and family practices are based. This more nuanced understanding of underlying processes, combined with Heymann's broader economic and social analysis, would, one hopes, increase the probability of effecting the change our society so desperately needs.

COSTS AND BENEFITS

WILLIAM A. GALSTON

I'm sympathetic to the basic thrust of Jody Heymann's argument. I would, however, rephrase the problem as follows: As a nation, we've done a reasonably good job of providing a public safety net for poor and near-poor families—roughly speaking, families with incomes below 150 percent of the federal poverty line—while families at or above the median income—roughly 300 percent of the poverty line—are typically able to meet basic needs through a combination of employer-provided benefits and services purchased out of earned income. But families in between—let's call them working-class—all too often lack access either to public programs or to employer benefits and cannot afford to plug the gap out of their earnings. As Heymann argues, this gap amounts to a denial of equal opportunity and has negative consequences for families and especially for children.

From a policy perspective, I would characterize Heymann's argument as moral and qualitative. She does not spend much time grappling with questions of program design and cost, or with issues of political coalition building and sustainability. Within these self-defined limits, her case is strong. Considerations of both social morality and long-term collective self-interest should lead us to respond aggressively. But not only should we do the right thing; we should do it in the right way. Below, I submit some guidelines for a sound strategy:

1. *Programs to assist working-class families must be compatible with vigorous long-term, noninflationary economic growth.* The second half of the 1990s witnessed a rapid increase in incomes across the board, coupled with a significant reduction in poverty. There is no substitute for sustainable tight labor markets, which under contemporary circumstances require sustainable fiscal discipline, as former treasury secretary Robert Rubin has rightly insisted.

2. *Programs to assist working-class families must also be compatible with rapid private sector job creation.* Consistent with this principle, we should avoid payroll taxes and employer mandates in favor of social provision based on general revenues. This strategy has the additional merit of emphasizing that society as a whole, not just a single sector, is responsible for fostering equal opportunity. For example, the federal government should enter into a fiscal partnership with the states to create a pool of funds for paid family leave.

3. *Considerations of both equity and affordability should direct us to means-tested programs as our basic model of provision for the working class.* Means-tested programs are not inherently feeble and endangered, as many social policy advocates have wrongly argued. Many

means-tested programs enjoy broad bipartisan support, and the most significant assault on working-class poverty in the past generation—President Clinton's dramatic expansion of the Earned Income Tax Credit—was pegged to family income. The best and fairest means-tested programs use sliding scales, with the largest subsidies for the worst-off families and phased-out benefits above a suitable income threshold.

4. *We should use measures of need as a basis of eligibility for government-provided services as well as income.* For example, research suggests that low-income and minority children stand to gain the most from educational reforms such as smaller class sizes and summer instruction. It would not be wise to rush toward universal programs in these areas, even if they were affordable (which they aren't). We should start where both the need and the return on social investment are the greatest.

5. *We should distinguish between the public sector as a provider of opportunities and as a provider of services and emphasize the former whenever possible.* For example, in order to create universal access to preschool for all four-year-olds, Georgia provides sliding-scale, income-based subsidies redeemable at all pre-K providers—public, private, and nonprofit—who comply with basic state requirements. (During the 2000 elec-

tion, then Vice President Gore proposed a federal-state partnership, backed by $5 billion in annual federal subsidies, to spread the Georgia model nationwide.)

A similar model could be used to ensure universal access to health insurance for working-class families; the federal government should define a percentage of income that each family is expected to contribute to its health care expenses and provide a subsidy to close the gap between that sum and the cost of a standard package of insurance benefits. The state would define basic requirements for private program eligibility to redeem these subsidies and would also allow families to buy into public programs such as Medicaid and CHIP.

6. *In designing programs to equalize opportunity, we must pay attention to research on quantifiable success and cost-effectiveness.* I do not read the evidence in quite the same way as Heymann does. For example, my years of teaching education policy have convinced me that the research basis for many popular reforms is weak at best. While certain "model programs" (Heymann's phrase) work very well, it's hard to know whether these programs would be as effective if scaled up. Much of the research on the long-term effectiveness of Head Start, for instance, revolves around the famous Perry Preschool experiment, which is far from the typical Head Start program.

In a political environment defined by shrinking federal budget surpluses and a return to deficits in the majority of the states, we must ask some hard questions about costs and benefits. In a perfect world, for example, the school year might well be forty days longer. But each additional day could cost as much as a billion dollars. If the measure of benefit is educational attainment, the evidence suggests that we could do better by investing scarce dollars in teacher training, recruitment, and retention.

I offer these comments as friendly policy amendments within Heymann's broad normative framework. I agree with her basic premise: justice in liberal democracies is the promise of equal opportunity, and we cannot say that working-class families in the United States enjoy that opportunity. If we are patient and smart, we can construct a coalition for fairness across party lines to implement an equal-opportunity program that public budgets and the private sector can sustain.

THE DISMAL SCIENCE

SUSAN MOLLER OKIN

Jody Heymann's account of the intensified reproduction of poverty in the United States and the reasons for it is very well informed, lucid, and alarming. The appalling paucity of care available to millions of children—including many of the worst-off economically—should be a national scandal. Having no disagreements with the case Heymann makes, I'll use this opportunity to make a point about the ideological background to the conditions she describes and to suggest that a very similar situation has emerged in much of the less developed and the formerly communist world. It is a problem endemic to late capitalism and the neoclassical economics that justifies its free-market extremism. The most important differences between the United States and these other, less economically advanced countries are that the disintegration of adequate care for children has come about much more quickly and rapidly there than here and that because of their economic vulnerability and debt, the governments of these countries had little choice about the matter.

One of the fundamental assumptions of the neoclassical brand of economics that now dominates the discipline is that only goods and services exchanged in the market have value. Having economic value, in turn, is necessary for something to be included in economic growth or the usual measure of such growth—per capita gross domestic product (GDP). The growth of per capita GDP is assumed to be not only a good thing but the normal indicator of a society's economic health—which is often assumed by politicians as well as economists to be the only kind of health that matters. Paid labor makes economies grow; thus the greater the numbers of people who work for pay or whose products are sold, and the more work they do, the healthier a country is considered to be. Unpaid labor, on the other hand, has no value. Thus when persons give up unpaid work and take up paid work, nothing of value is lost. Moreover, when persons who are not paid take on more unpaid work than they did previously, no more work is undertaken. Indeed, when people take up and do for no pay what was previously paid for by governments, great savings can be made, and nothing of value is lost.

Finally, neoclassical economists have long assumed (though some are now questioning) that even though households usually consist of a number of individuals, each household can be treated as if it were a single individual. Thus, from an economist's point of view, a household in which one adult member goes out to a full-time job that pays $X and the other stays home to do unpaid work (such as housework, child care, or nursing the sick or old) is identical to a household in which both adult members work full time for a combined income of $X. So, also, is a household in which the member who used to work for pay becomes unemployed and does nothing, while the one who does the unpaid work continues to do it while taking on a job that pays $X.

Many connections exist between these assumptions and the serious problems discussed in Jody Heymann's essay. For while the assumptions economists make may bear little relation to the ways most of us see the world, they are translated into policies (or the absence of policies). And when they are, they have a great deal of bearing on the world. In the United States, the lack of valuation of women's unpaid work contributed heavily to justifying the so-called welfare reform legislation of 1996. For since women at home with children (excepting, perhaps, those with rich husbands) were not considered to be doing anything of value, it was easy to portray them as irresponsible loafers and push them and their children even further below the poverty line than they already were. Now that these "welfare mothers" are required to "work," states have discovered that paying other women to take care of these children can actually be more expensive than it was to enable these mothers to care for their own children at home. Perhaps, eventually, as child care becomes a market commodity, it may garner more legitimacy and respect—though indications so far are that it will be far from highly valued. (We pay zoo workers far more than we pay those who care for infants and toddlers and those who teach small children.) Similar to the current lack of support for the single parents of small children is the lack of comprehensive or paid family and medical leave (even given the

Family Medical Leave Act of 1993), a problem that Heymann analyzes so well. This too owes much to the same ideology of hypercapitalism in which what is not a marketable commodity has no value.

As a result of U.S. economic power during the last two decades of the twentieth century, the problems exacerbated by this neoclassical outlook have become far more prevalent in many economically disadvantaged countries. For what was happening in the latest stage of capitalism in this country was translated into the Structural Adjustment Policies that the World Bank and International Monetary Fund have pushed on all governments with high levels of international debt. Fundamental to these institutions' vision of an economically healthy, "developed" rest-of-the-world was the unfettered operation of free markets. Thus governments of indebted countries were urged and pressured to lift import duties and restrictions, to stop subsidizing infant industries and basic food staples, to balance their budgets (though not to stop buying arms), and as part of this cost saving to charge "user fees" for public services such as education and health care.

These policies have had deleterious effects on both women and children. Free trade and the elimination of subsidies had the effect of eliminating jobs that were in many cultural contexts typically or even exclusively done by men, such as heavy manufacturing, and substituting jobs typically or even exclusively done by women, such as microchip manufacturing, sewing clothes, and other jobs requiring small motor skills (and, often, subordination to authority). Since for economists jobs at the same skill level are fungible, they can have no gender. But in the real world, where the economists' policies are applied, men often become unemployed while women become newly employed and still take care of the home and children—for culture does not change as fast as markets do. The budget balancing that has been demanded of indebted countries, in some cases, explicitly depends on increasing women's unpaid work. In a policy move that is called cost-shifting, hospital and other health care cuts are recommended, with the explicit expectation that women will take up the work of caring for the sick that had been previously funded by the state. Needless to say, the health care and the education of children of both sexes, but especially that of girls, suffered or at the very least failed to progress, because of the inability of hundreds of millions of people to pay the user fees that were charged for these services.

It is, as the story Heymann tells makes clear, unconscionable that in the United States, with all its wealth, children—and especially the children of the economically least well off—should be suffering such lack of care. Why we should be so careless of the nutrition, the physical and psychological health, and the education of so many of the country's future citizens seems incomprehensible. Indifference to the fate of most of the world's people seems to be an increasingly acceptable mode of thought in the contemporary United States. But what are we assuming about the future of our own country—which we presumably do care about, at some level? Do we think there will be an endless influx of healthy, educated immigrants from the middle and upper classes of other nations, to substitute for and to support all the illiterate and dysfunctional people we are creating through our failure to ensure care for children? Quite apart from issues of equity and human decency, Heymann is right to point out that it even makes economic sense—except in the immediate short run—to do things very differently. How long will it take us to break out of the mold of neoclassical economic thinking that has so contributed to this mess?

STRENGTH IN NUMBERS

KAREN NUSSBAUM

When my children were little, getting them out the door to the day care center and myself and my husband to work on time was a major mobilization. "Hurry, hurry, hurry," I urged in a voice a little too loud. "We're late, we're late, we're late!" Months into this ritual, my middle child asked me, "Mom, what does 'late' mean?" *A-ha*, I thought. Maybe this isn't a problem of will—he just hasn't understood me!

I have often thought of this when considering the inertia of employers and politicians when it comes to establishing meaningful work and family policies. Maybe we just have not expressed the need clearly. But Jody Heymann's careful research and compelling argument cap a growing body of work over the last twenty years with incontrovertible conclusions: our failure as a nation to provide essential work/family supports seriously harms parents and their children, especially those who are poor.

"Listen to my words," child care teachers admonish their charges. Work and family advocates have been articulate— what we have lacked is power. Where workers have power through a collective voice on the job—a union—they are more likely to have the kind of relief that Heymann calls for. The good news is that unions are turning more attention to these issues.

Ask a Working Woman

Working parents echo the findings in Heymann's research and tell us that the problems faced by families go far beyond the poor. In the AFL-CIO's *Ask a Working Woman 2000 Survey*, a representative sample of all working women told us of the strains on their families: two-thirds of women with children at home work full time; more than one out of four women work nights or weekends as part of their regularly scheduled workweeks; and nearly half of all women work different schedules than their spouses or partners do.

While their work hours wreak havoc with these families—Harriet Presser of the University of Maryland reports higher divorce rates for couples who work different shifts—workers are getting little relief from their employers. Nearly one-third of working women say they do not even have paid sick leave *for themselves;* more than half have no paid leave to care for a baby or ill family member; and one-third have no flexibility or control over their work hours. Yet workers believe they are entitled to these benefits. A recent survey ("Workers' Rights in America," conducted by the AFL-CIO in September 2001) indicated that 90 percent of workers consider it essential or very important to have time off to care for a baby or sick family member and 90 percent believe workers are entitled to sick leave.

Say What?

Few advocates realize the importance of unions in winning reasonable work and family policies. Workers who belong to unions are more likely to have the working conditions that the vast majority of workers feel entitled to. For example, long before the federal government passed family and medical leave legislation, many union workers enjoyed job-protected parental leave. A study of collective bargaining agreements in SEIU and AFSCME in the late 1980s found that more than 80 percent of contracts provided parental leave.

In a 1998 study by the Families and Work Institute, companies with 30 percent or more unionized workers were far more likely than nonunion companies to provide the following: paid time off to care for sick children (65 percent compared with 46 percent); fully paid family health insurance (40 percent compared with 8 percent); temporary disability insurance (87 percent compared with 66 percent); and pensions (79 percent compared with 40 percent). Union representation is one of the strongest predictors of good work and family benefits.

TALK THE TALK, WALK THE WALK

Unions have a long history of struggling to make work respond to family needs: from the fight to limit the workweek 150 years ago, to the network of child care centers set up by the Amalgamated Clothing and Textile Workers Union in the 1960s (which made them the biggest private-sector provider of child care at the time), to the groundbreaking contracts in the last two decades that confronted an array of work and family issues in almost every industry, with the most impressive gains in the auto industry, telecommunications, and the public sector.

Today, more than ever, unions are fighting for progress on core issues such as work hours, paid leave, and child care in collective bargaining and public policy. Here are a few examples:

> The United American Nurses has gone on strike nearly fifty times in the last three years over the issue of staffing and mandatory overtime.

> Seventy-two thousand members of the Communications Workers of America struck Verizon in 2000 to secure limits on mandatory overtime.

> In a $60 million program that sets the new high-water mark, the United Auto Workers recently opened the first of thirty-one Family Service and Education Centers with the Ford Motor Company. Many of the centers will include twenty-four-hour child care, tax planning, home repair classes, self-defense and driver's education classes, book clubs, walking clubs, day trips for seniors, and vocational and career assessment.

> A dozen state federations of labor are backing state legislation that mandates paid family leave.

The New York Union Child Care Coalition successfully lobbied the state legislature to add hundreds of
millions of dollars for child care to the state budget.

Sandra Feldman, president of the American Federation of Teachers, announced a commitment to work
for universal access to preschool as a matter of
national policy.

At its 2001 convention, the AFL-CIO passed the
"Respect Work, Strengthen Family" resolution,
which calls for a wide range of improvements in
work and family policies.

SAY IT ISN'T SO

Unions are essential in building the power base that work
and family advocates like Jody Heymann need to make real
change. Andy Stern, president of SEIU, pointing to the 40
to 50 percent wage differential enjoyed by low-wage union
workers, often argues that unionization is the most effective
antipoverty program in the United States—and it doesn't
cost the government a dime. The same can be said about the
role of unions in creating more family-friendly workplaces
and public policies.

It stands to reason that work and family advocates have a
stake in the continued success of unions. Yet workers who

choose to take control of their own working lives by unionizing are thwarted every day. A study published in 2000 by Cornell University's Kate Bronfenbrenner found, among other forms of intimidation, that employers illegally fire union supporters in 31 percent of organizing campaigns, and half of employers threaten to shut down the company if employees join a union.

So, as we join together to promote the essential family supports that Heymann calls for, we need to ensure the inviolable right of workers to meet their family needs by organizing on the job.

BEYOND OPPORTUNITY

ISABELLE FERRERAS

I agree with Jody Heymann's description of the present state of U.S. social policy, in particular its treatment of working-class and poor parents and their children—treatment that becomes increasingly disgraceful as one descends the uniquely unequal American income ladder. And I agree, also, with her description of a more ameliorative social policy for working families. But I am less confident that the equal opportunity idea that she cites at the start of her essay provides the critical leverage that she needs.

Gunnar Myrdal said that the American credo comprises a short list of common beliefs including the "dear belief that all people have an equal opportunity . . . an equal chance at succeeding . . . if one works hard." Heymann suggests that a better deal can be achieved for working families by wrapping policy demands in the language of this "dear belief." The credo is sound: what we need to do is modernize its realization in light of changed family structures, work arrangements, and the like. Because the value of equal opportunity is widely shared, it is a rhetorical strategy that might plausibly help organize needed political support, as well as provide a principled basis for judging policy alternatives.

But precisely because the rhetoric of equal opportunity

is so widely shared—by progressives and conservatives alike—the message may not be very effective. Equal opportunity has now become something of a political mantra and may serve more as a smokescreen than as a useful guide to policy. One must not forget how deeply moving Governor Bush was during his 2000 campaign as he promised to offer to all American children an equal opportunity to live out the American dream.

In reality, no current U.S. policy initiative truly embodies the principle of equal opportunity in the real life of American working parents and their children, at least when compared with equal opportunity programs in European welfare states. The situation described by Heymann is a confirmation of the fact that social and economic rights have never been seriously extended to U.S. citizens. Perhaps in the end the equal opportunity principle is a matter of rhetorical commitment more than practical credo. Perhaps it is time to rethink the principle itself.

That rethinking should start with a shift of attention from *opportunity* to *capability*. The concept of capabilities, developed by Amartya Sen and Martha Nussbaum, takes into consideration the scope of a person's available choices: the alternatives that a person could pursue if he or she chose, as opposed to those that are permissible but not really available. It is not only a semantic change, but also a change of focus: it looks at one's real chances in dealing with the various requirements of life (working, family, etc.) in a fair way.

Founding a vision of social justice on a conception of rights in terms of opportunity does not seem suitable for today's challenges. Indeed freedom of choice is not merely a matter of personal virtue, individual opportunity, and private resources. Nor is it a simple matter of substantive redistribution through state policies. Instead, it depends importantly on the ability to coordinate actions with other people.[1] A capability-based approach to social justice may allow us to address the collective dimension of social life that appears decisive in today's situation.

Indeed, to tackle the problems of working families caused by the new patterns of work in our capitalist postindustrial societies, we need to reconfigure regulatory practices. In today's world of flexible work and fragile democracy, state regulation should seek to build a new public framework to provide real means for citizens to act together. Looking for ways to improve capabilities of citizens to pursue joint actions requires taking the collective dimension of life (and thus democracy) into consideration.[2] In policy terms, this not only implies that working parents deserve days of paid family leave and that elderly and disabled adults deserve opportunities and anti-age-discrimination policies in the workplace. It means that they all deserve true *capabilities* to meet, discuss, and be partners in decisions regarding their own lives (i.e., at work and at school) and also regarding areas of common concern (public administration, health, transportation, and so on). That is the meaning of collective rights, both social and economic.

Applied to policy, this strategy would mean not only providing more funding for schools, particularly those serving underprivileged populations, but also—drawing some examples from the Belgian experience, which I know best—setting up participatory boards (Belgium's *Conseils de participation*) where pupils or their delegates meet with the different school stakeholders and participate in defining the many aspects of life at school (from the educational project to the need to get a smoking section in the cafeteria). For clerks the strategy would mean participating in a team (Belgium's *ilots-caisses*) that can negotiate individual schedules based on the specific needs of both the employer (opening hours, sales requirements, number of patrons, etc.) and their family lives. By pooling employees with different backgrounds (single mothers, students, older people without children), this mode of work organization—under the supervision of both the employer and union representatives—gives employees the opportunity to reclaim their own capacity for organizing their lives out of work while addressing their employer's need for flexibility. For those living on welfare, the strategy would bring beneficiaries together on a local basis in committees (Belgium's *Comités d'usagers*) to help define their own needs and to engage in important acts of self-definition and negotiation.

At a time when the state is no longer able to address every single problem, much less imagine and enforce a solution, it is of crucial importance to equip all citizens with the capabilities to participate in society. And securing this participation is essential if "we the people" want to live in an effective democracy.

THE RIGHT TIME

THOMAS A. KOCHAN

Americans need a new set of family-centered labor market policies and institutions if we are to address the problems facing working families that Jody Heymann documents so clearly and eloquently. The policies and institutions governing work today are better suited to the industrial economy of the New Deal era. The typical worker of that time was assumed to be a male breadwinner in a long-term career with a large company earning a wage sufficient to support his family. However, today women account for half the workforce; less than 20 percent of families consist of a male breadwinner with a wife at home; employment durations are both shorter and more uncertain; and work takes place in a wide variety of small and large firms, in independent contractor/consultant relationships, and in multiple locations including the home. The failure to update policies and institutions to fit these new realities of work and family life is a major reason why, as Heymann argues, it is nearly impossible for lower-income working families to succeed both at work and in caring for their families.

What would such an updated view of labor market policies and institutions look like? Consider just one piece of the puzzle: how to provide all working families with paid leave that could be used in a flexible fashion to meet the different types of family needs encountered at different stages of one's family life cycle.[1] Heymann rightly views the provision of some form of paid time off to care for children and family needs as the basic building block of any family-centered labor market policy. She notes that while many in the upper half of family income distribution can draw on vacation, sick leave, or flexible working hours to attend to family needs without loss of pay, the majority of low-paid workers lack access to any form of paid time off for these purposes. The policy challenge is how to extend these benefits to the working poor without duplicating them for those already covered and without imposing rigid and costly requirements that are poorly tailored to the variety of family needs people experience at different stages of their careers.

One way to do this would be to create a set of minimum standards (Heymann proposes the equivalent of two weeks paid leave per year) while allowing employers and employees considerable flexibility in how to integrate this leave with existing policies and practices. Individuals could be encouraged to set up flexible time accounts analogous to 401K plans or individual retirement accounts. These accounts could be (1) *flexible,* so that they could be used for any family care needs; (2) *accruable* to the individual, so that unused days saved in one year carry over into the future; (3) *portable,* so that the dollar equivalents of unused leave move with an employee across job changes; and (4) *contributory,* so that individuals could choose to allocate some portion of current vacation or sick leave to this purpose in the current period or match employer contributions to their accounts with pretax salary deductions.

Updating leave policies to make this approach work would require corresponding changes within key labor market institutions as well in the relationships among them at the workplace, community, and national levels. Unions and professional associations, for example, could sponsor and administer these plans. They would need to offer their members continuous, lifetime memberships that are not dependent on whether a collective bargaining relationship exists on their current jobs. Within firms, peer employees, supervisors, and managers would need to work together to redesign work and encourage use of flexible time benefits in ways that promote efficiency and fairness and that protect caregivers from stigmatization and career damage. Some form of community-level Working Family Councils would also be needed to support both these workplace innovations and the range of improvements in transportation, education, and other social institutions that Heymann rightly argues are necessary to make the American Dream accessible to the children of today's working families. These regional groups could then come together annually in a National Working Families Summit to take stock of the nation's progress in meeting these needs.

Still, we must ask, is this all unrealistic? After all, labor policies have been stalled by a political impasse between labor and business for over thirty years, and the current focus on the international war on terrorism means that these issues have been pushed even further off the national agenda. I believe it is possible to make political progress, but only if we begin to see work and family policies as tightly coupled components of a progressive social policy agenda. I believe the American public is ready to support innovative proposals that respond to the realities of work and family as they experience them today—proposals that bypass the single-earner model of the New Deal era. Not only does the American public need a family-centered labor market policy—it is ready and waiting for one to be proposed. Any leader who has the courage to do so will unleash a groundswell of political support and reap its benefits for a long time to come.

SHARING THE BURDEN

MYRA MARX FERREE

Are you as tired as I am of hearing how all the problems of U.S. families—and especially those of American children—can be traced back to women entering the labor force? Even more tiresome is the customary conclusion that this one change in women's typical life course is responsible for putting stress on husbands and children, even leading to a supposed breakdown of the family. Implicit in this view, of course, is the idea that because women "caused" the problems of the two-job family, it is now women's obligation to solve them, whether by retreating to the home, restricting themselves to underpaid part-time jobs in order to better balance their "traditional" home and family responsibilities, or by rising to the task of being superwomen who can carry the burdens of a full-time job and a family life.

Jody Heymann offers a welcome respite from such women-blaming. She points out that transformations in the economy drew *both* men and women into the industrial labor force at different times and speeds, whereas the stereotypical picture of men out "at work" and women "at home" (and implicitly not working) is simply wrong. It is worth repeating her point, that over the past 150 years farm families turned into wage-earning families, as *both* women and men sought out new and better ways to provide what their house-holds needed, both to survive and to get ahead.

But in fact the transformation is not only in adult lives but also in children's. As the much lower high school graduation rates before World War II suggest, and as many people still alive today remember, children were not so long ago active members in the family economy. For many families struggling to get by in the first half of the twentieth century, the preferred method of supplementing income was to pull children out of school and send them to work, whether in factories or as messengers, as vendors, or as workers in the earliest service industries (from shoe shining to domestic service).[1] Almost twenty years ago, historian Mary Ryan's study of nineteenth-century New York showed how the shift toward an economy in which children required more education to succeed precipitated new demands on women to provide it, whether by tutoring their youngest children or by paying high school fees and college tuitions for their older ones.[2]

Long before married women's work began to shift toward paid labor, it had already changed dramatically, from providing the physical labor and material goods that early-twentieth-century households required to providing the educational and developmental support that modern children need. Academic achievement, not inheritance of a share in the family farm or business, is the means by which nearly all middle-class families expect their children to equal or surpass their own standard of living. Fostering children's academic achievement is therefore the strategy modern families follow to push them ahead in life, and only the poorest and most desperate families are tempted to pull their children out of school. Married women work to support their children's schooling and future achievements, no less than children once labored for pay so that their mothers could stay home and do the arduous labor required to keep the household running.

In other words, except for the brief interlude between about 1945 and 1960—when men's wages were exceptionally high, when income inequality was unusually low, when most men were already absorbed into the paid economy and most married mothers were not yet there—"the past" and "the traditional family" look nothing at all like our customary picture of it. Women, men, and children worked. Beaver Cleaver is a historical anomaly. By pointing to the costs that inflexible jobs and agricultural-era school patterns impose on children's ability to learn and succeed in school, Heymann mobilizes the real essence of contemporary family values: get the kids the best education you can. It is also a challenge to the pseudo-family-values discourse that is one of the greatest obstacles to creating the changes she calls for.

In fact, blaming women, feminism, or the decline in patriarchal authority for the problems families face is the favorite tactic of those who do not want states to spend a nickel to help them out. On this view, if women take responsibility in a new economy and "choose" to work, then women should somehow, personally and privately, find solutions to every new problem the family faces. In reality, women are indeed taking up the lion's share of the day-to-day personal and economic burden of "juggling" responsibilities that are still so often described as theirs alone. By casting women and choice as the root of the problem, the blame for society's failure to address family needs can be shifted to the women's movement and away from the political parties, interest groups, and voters who have failed to demand the kinds of sensible mediating mechanisms that Heymann calls for.[3]

The missing link in Heymann's argument is the political one. The flexibility and social support that she calls on public bureaucracies, schools, and workplaces to offer are not free, even if they are more affordable than most Americans assume. But then, in the 1920s and 1930s the introduction of such measures as social security, unemployment insurance, and job-based health insurance did not fall from the sky either. There were active social movements campaigning for government to provide "mother's pensions" and pensions for the elderly. Only after years of struggle, including confrontational "movement" politics, lobbying, and get-out-the-vote drives, were these demands answered with policy concessions.[4] The women's movement had a role to play then, as it did in winning the FMLA and as it still does today. But any serious hope of achieving these reasonable accommodations to the modern realities of our families, our economy, and our educational system demands that we stop viewing women as the sole bearers of responsibility for caregiving in the family and for social progress in our institutions.

A NEW VISION

BRADLEY K. GOOGINS

Jody Heymann's essay opens an important discussion about the barriers faced by working parents and the failures of public policies and institutions to provide caregivers with a basic level of support. American efforts to address these issues reveal both the strengths and weaknesses of our society. The prevailing values of self-reliance, privacy, and family— so essential to the early development of the United States— no longer serve the needs of working families. Self-reliance in an era of complex economic environments, demanding workplaces, diminishing public supports, and deteriorating community infrastructure does little to ensure that basic family needs are met. Unlike virtually every other developed country across the globe, issues of child care, elder care, education, and health in the United States are generally perceived to be the province of the individual and the family, and government policy on families is virtually nonexistent.

Recently corporations have taken the lead in creating a series of innovative programs and policy responses to address the needs of working families. Sometimes referred to as "family-friendly companies," a number of leading businesses have established a wide array of very powerful and popular supports for families ranging from on-site child care to concierge services—policies that may give families more time to take care of needs like early childhood education, not to mention dry cleaning and car maintenance. While these benefits have been quite successful in addressing the needs of beneficiaries, their limits again reflect our national values and biases. Only the very small percentage of working parents who happen to be employed by these (generally large and prosperous) corporations have access to these supports.

And there lies the rub. By placing responsibility for such basic needs as child care and looking after our elders exclusively on the individual and family, we have created a system that relies on the good fortunes of individual families, or the good fortunes of those who work for family-friendly companies. In today's world of highly mobile families where most adults work and indeed have to work to meet basic needs, traditional methods of mutual aid by families and communities are less viable. So who should take responsibility for the care of dependents and guarantee that our families and communities are, at a basic level, healthy and sustainable?

What we have now is a clouded vision and fragmented policies for addressing the needs of working families. We cannot imagine a society (like those of Europe) where government and employers work collaboratively to ensure the most basic supports and design policies conducive to healthy and sustainable family life. In the United States, corporate policy and public policy generally work at cross-purposes, with free marketers fending off regulation and legislative mandates. Caught in between are working families, who at the end of the day are still running as fast as they can to assemble a patchwork of informal and formal supports, unable to rely to any great extent on the public or private sector to help them meet their basic family needs.

What, then, would a family-friendly community look like? Might there not be mechanisms whereby multiple stakeholders in the community such as schools, churches, local governments, civic associations, and businesses all come together to create a place where families and children could thrive? Is it really too utopian to imagine such a place, especially since it is ultimately in the interests of all for such collaboration to occur? Business depends on healthy families and communities in order to sustain productivity, investment, and growth. One need only look to the growing involvement of business in public education to see how effective and popular such collaboration could be.

As frustration with current policies and stress levels for working families rise, such creative action is becoming more crucial. Despite the past decade of family-friendly programs, reported stress on families and individuals continues to increase, working hours are on the rise, and the corporate treadmill seems to be moving faster than ever.

We need an innovative vision for our families and our workplaces: a new vision of work and family and new roles for both the public and private sector. In the private sector, family needs have been conceptually and practically lodged within a human resources framework, defined and operationalized as an individual benefit, much like health care coverage or a pension. A more sustainable strategy might be to link its supports for working families to the new model of corporate citizenship. In partnerships with community institutions and local and state governments, businesses could capitalize on the strengths of public, private, and community sectors and force each to understand and value the assets and contributions of the others.

In the public sector, it is time to develop a concept of the family-friendly community that parallels that of the family-friendly company. Currently the private sector has exercised the primary leadership in developing supports for families, inventions mothered by the necessity of meeting the bottom line. The time has come for the public sector to share the mantle of leadership on family issues by placing the needs of working families at the top of the national priorities. Private solutions alone will not sustain the needs of working families.

AFFORDABLE POLICIES

JODI GRANT

The Family and Medical Leave Act (FMLA) was the first, and to date is the only, federal legislation to provide job protection for workers who face pressing family obligations. Prior to its enactment, Americans risked losing their jobs if they became seriously ill or chose to take time off to care for a newborn child or a loved one with a serious health condition. Since its passage, over 35 million American families have taken family and or medical leave.[1]

Some employers have realized that family-friendly benefits and working conditions are beneficial—not only for employees but for the business bottom line as well. Often the resources saved in retention and health care costs are well worth the expense of providing paid leave and flexible hours. However, most employers still do not provide these benefits, leaving workers struggling to balance their work and family obligations.

The FMLA provides up to twelve weeks of unpaid, job-protected leave per year to covered and eligible employees. Employees can take this leave upon the birth or adoption of a child or the placement of a foster child. They are also eligible for family and medical leave to recover from their own serious health conditions or to take care of a sick child, spouse, or parent. In order to be eligible for FMLA leave, however, an employee must have worked for an employer for the past twelve months and for at least 1,250 hours. In addition, the business must employ at least fifty employees within a seventy-five-mile radius of the employee's work site.

Even if eligible, millions of workers are still forced to choose between a paycheck and caring for a loved one. Of the men and women who take FMLA leave, 34 percent take it without any pay, and 78 percent of eligible employees who needed but did not take family or medical leave did not take it because they could not afford it.[2] One quarter of all sustained family struggles with poverty in the United States begin with the birth of a child.[3] And nearly one in ten leave-takers who receive less than full pay while on leave is forced onto public assistance.[4] Therefore paid leave must be made available to more American workers.

Low-income workers are disproportionately hurt. They are the least likely to have any paid leave and the most likely to lack savings. Of those in the lowest income quartile, 76 percent lack sick leave and 58 percent lack vacation leave.[5] For those workers who have sick leave, few can use it to care for family members. In addition, only 31 percent of women have paid maternity leave, and these tend to be highly educated professionals. Of women with a bachelor's degree or higher, 63 percent used paid benefits for maternity leave, compared with 18 percent of women who did not have a high school diploma.[6]

Jody Heymann highlights the public and private benefits

of taking family and medical leave. Patients who are cared for by family members have faster recoveries, providing significant savings on health care costs. Many child care facilities won't even consider admitting an infant before he or she is ten or twelve weeks old because the newborn's immune system is not yet mature, making the infant highly susceptible to infection. Time with parents is critical to a child's development and allows a baby to learn to trust and bond with the mother and/or father. For these reasons, almost every other industrialized nation provides paid parental leave. The average length of paid leave in European countries is ten months.[7] And in some developing countries, such as Afghanistan prior to Taliban rule, working mothers received ninety days of paid maternity leave.[8]

OPPOSITION

Members of the business community, most notably the Chamber of Commerce and the National Federation of Independent Businesses, vigorously opposed the original Family and Medical Leave Act. They argued that a government mandate would wreak havoc on business productivity and profitability. Studies have proved them wrong. A 2000 Labor Department survey found that 90 percent of businesses reported either no additional costs or showed actual savings as a result of family and medical leave policies, and 84 percent of businesses covered by the FMLA found that it either increased or had no impact on productivity.[9]

Yet the same criticism of the original Family and Medical Leave Act is being used to argue against paid leave, with businesses claiming that it will have a disastrous effect on productivity and profitability. In reality, the cost of providing paid leave is relatively low, and the benefits are high. Businesses benefit from decreased health care costs and increased retention. In fact, 94 percent of fully paid leave-takers return to the same employer after taking leave.[10] A recent Census Bureau report confirmed that paid leave has a stronger retention effect than unpaid leave.[11] Studies have confirmed that the costs of hiring a new employee (such as advertising, interviewing, and training) are far greater than the cost of providing short-term leave to retain existing employees. This holds true for low-income employees as well as highly paid and skilled professionals.[12]

In addition to business benefits, there are important impacts on public health. Sick children recover faster if their parents care for them. Infants that stay at home for the first few weeks are less likely to contract dangerous infections. If sick children and parents stay at home, they are less likely to pass their illness on to others. Heymann's research demonstrates that the public benefit goes even further, as she uncovers a direct correlation between a parent's access to paid leave and a child's academic performance.

For these reasons, state and federal policy makers have sought to create programs to provide paid leave. The most expansive proposals provide a financial safety net for women and men on family or medical leave. Others provide income replacement for new parents. A third approach allows employees to use their accrued sick leave to take care of family members.

These proposals are not expensive. Some of the legislative proposals are funded entirely by state surpluses or state-budgeted child care funds. Others require employer and/or employee contributions. For example, a Vermont proposal for paid parental leave was estimated to cost fifteen cents per worker per week, and a Washington state proposal for paid family leave was estimated to cost two cents per employee for each hour worked.

AFFORDABLE APPROACHES

State legislators are leading the way on innovative proposals to provide paid family leave. In 2001, family leave benefit bills were introduced in twenty-six states, and nineteen state legislatures held hearings on providing paid family leave. Governor Howard Dean (D–Vt.) and Governor Jane Swift (R–Mass.) also introduced plans to provide paid parental leave.

Oklahoma enacted legislation that allows state employees to use their accrued sick leave to take care of sick family members. Employees are also permitted to donate unused accrued leave to a coworker in need. This allows employees to receive paid family and medical leave as well as paid leave to take care of a child, spouse, or parent who is not seriously ill but needs to see a doctor or is home sick. This program has no impact on the state budget and may be an attractive way for policy makers to assist working families during an economic downturn.

Some states, like California, have gone further, requiring all employers that provide sick leave to allow employees to use it to care for a sick child, spouse, or parent. Montana recently created a program modeled after Minnesota's At Home Infant Care Program. Both programs, geared toward low-income parents, allow eligible parents to receive designated child care funds to stay at home for the first year of a child's life. There is no additional financial burden placed on state budgets, because these programs rely on funds that have already been budgeted.

Five states—California, Hawaii, New Jersey, New York, and Rhode Island, as well Puerto Rico—have provided paid leave for some types of family and medical leave for over forty years through their Temporary Disability Insurance programs. These programs provide coverage to employees suffering from non-job-related injuries or illnesses as well as maternity-related disability. Employers and/or employees pay for the program. In some states the program is run by a state agency. In others, employers contract privately to provide the benefits. Benefits range from a minimum of $170 a week in New York to $492 a week in California. Approximately 65 percent of the people in these states who need family and medical leave are entitled to paid leave because of these temporary disability laws. New York, New Jersey,

California, and Hawaii have all introduced legislative proposals to expand their disability leave to cover other types of family and medical leave.

Other states have proposed the creation of family leave funds, the use of state surplus dollars, or the expansion of unemployment insurance programs to provide paid parental leave.

FEDERAL PROPOSALS

Federal legislators have recognized these promising state proposals and have introduced legislation to authorize 400 million dollars in direct grants to states to provide funding for paid family leave pilot programs. These proposals have been included in the top bills introduced by the Democratic leadership in both the House and the Senate. Federal legislators are considering a bill that would require employers to provide a minimum amount of paid leave for all employees that could be used for their own illnesses, for care of sick loved ones, and for medical visits, school visits, continuing education, and so on.

All of these promising new initiatives continue to gain momentum despite the current economic downturn. It is instructive to note that the Family and Medical Leave Act was passed shortly after unemployment hit a high of 7.5 percent in 1992.[13] In times of recession, the public is more concerned than ever about job protection, and the strain to balance family and work becomes even more pronounced.

Changing Demographics

Public support for paid leave is overwhelming. A recent national poll found that 89 percent of parents of young children and 84 percent of all adults support paid parental leave.[14] And this need will only continue to grow. In 1997, one in four Americans had an elderly relative to care for, and many reduced their work hours or took at least a brief leave to care for that person.[15] Nearly two-thirds of American women and men under the age of sixty believe they will have to care for an older relative in the next decade.[16]

Since the 1970s, more and more women have entered the workforce and the need for paid leave for both men and women has become an increasingly important family issue. In 1998, 51 percent of married couples with children both worked, up from 33 percent in 1976. In 1998, 59 percent of women with babies younger than age one were employed, up from 31 percent in 1976.[17]

As with the original Family and Medical Leave Act, it will take time to pass legislation that makes paid leave a reality for more American families. The strong support for family leave benefits continues to grow, and more and more policy makers are determined to find ways to provide their constituents with a safety net. It is only a matter of time before American workers, like those in most of the rest of the world, will be entitled to some income for family or medical leave.

POLICY MATTERS

FRANCES FOX PIVEN

I endorse Jody Heymann's program. I especially appreciate her concern with the caretaking work on which family well-being depends. It is a concern not much heard on the Left, with the consequence that popular anxieties about stressed families have largely been captured by right-wing moralists who attribute family troubles to the immoral conduct of those afflicted.

Still, I think something is missing from Heymann's chronicle of how these troubles developed and, relatedly, from her agenda for reform. The problems of American families are not just the result of our failure as a nation to adapt to a changing economy and its changing workforce requirements. It is true of course that employment has shifted from agriculture to industry and from home-based work for women to paid labor. But this has occurred virtually everywhere in the world, including the European countries that Heymann points to as exemplars of the family and child-oriented policies she favors.

What is different in the United States is not simply that it is laggard in developing public supports of family caretaking functions. Beyond that, the United States has pioneered policies in the workplace and in public policy that erode the caretaking capacities of families. The past few decades have witnessed an extraordinary intensification of wage work in the United States, which is characterized not only by the movement of women into the paid workforce (often a response to declines in men's earnings), but also by longer working hours for men and women alike and the spread of new and insecure forms of employment, including temporary, contingent, or contracted work.

This is a development of historic proportions. The whiggish American expectation that over time things get better, wages rise, hours get shorter and vacations longer has been exploded. But it is not simply a consequence of changes in the economy, of the growth of the service sector and the decline of manufacturing, for example, or of intensified international competition. If it were, then workers in all rich countries would confront similar conditions: the five-week vacation would be a thing of the past in Germany, and France would not be experimenting with a shortened workweek. Instead the intensification of wage work has been facilitated in the United States by a series of reversals in established public policies, each of which has been justified as a necessary adaptation to contemporary economic conditions.

Some of these policies affect the ability of American workers to organize collectively. Thus most everyone agrees that labor unions not only secure higher wages but also enable workers to resist forced overtime and irregular work schedules. In the United States, unions are now in retreat, their memberships shrinking to pre-1930s levels. And just as the rise of unions in the 1930s reflected the new government protection of the right to organize embodied in the National Labor Relations Act, so does the decline of unions, and the consequent inability of workers to resist the imposition of new and harsher workplace policies, reflect the long-term gutting of the National Labor Relations Act.

The slashing or erosion of other public programs also contributes to the more demanding conditions of wage work. One of the benefits of the unemployment insurance program introduced in the 1930s was that it reduced the desperation of laid-off workers, making it less likely that they would have to settle for a job with lower pay and worse working conditions. But today the program reaches only 40 percent of the unemployed, and a far smaller percentage of workers who were laid off from low-wage jobs. The evisceration of programs that provide low-cost housing or nutritional supports for low-income families also makes the unemployed more desperate and forces those who are employed to scramble for more hours of work to compensate for reduced public supports.

The most dramatic change in public policy that contributes to the intensification of work and the erosion of caretaking occurred in welfare policy. Welfare was traditionally understood as a program to make it possible for single mothers to care for their children. Now many of these women have been forced into the low-wage labor market, with scant provision for the double burdens they carry as workers and caregivers. Moreover, "welfare reform" has turned into a great dramaturgical production, celebrating wage work and denigrating the work that these women did as caretakers of their families.

Some erstwhile defenders of welfare have argued that there were in fact compensations, that welfare reform smoothed the way for policies to support low-wage workers, such as the expansion of the Earned Income Tax Credit (EITC), and presumably for the sorts of programs Heymann recommends. But we should be cautious here. It is a good thing, of course, that the EITC increases the earnings of low-wage families. This, however, will be of little comfort to the women who followed the welfare-to-work path only to find themselves unemployed when the labor market slackened. In the battle for family-oriented policies, it is important to remember that work-conditioned social programs—whether tax credits or child care supports or pensions or health benefits—always increase the power of employers over workers, because they allow employers to threaten not only employment and wages, but an array of other protections. Consider, for instance, the plight of Enron workers who recently lost their pensions as well as their jobs when the firm collapsed.

So, yes. We want policies that support family caretaking, and Heymann's agenda is reasonable. These programs should not be restricted to working families but should reach all children and adults in need—partly because otherwise the poor who are marginal to the labor force will be excluded, with pernicious effects for them, and ultimately for all of us. We should avoid work conditioning for another reason, because one of the principles behind public supports is precisely that they can loosen the yoke of employers on workers.

That agreed, a family-oriented social policy agenda should be broader. We should go beyond public programs that supplement specific family caregiving functions to reevaluate the policies that are eroding the caregiving capacities of families in the first place. It is unlikely that Heymann's ambitious agenda will be enacted any time soon, but even if it is, these programs can only partially compensate for the betrayal of the labor and public policy standards on which adequate caregiving ultimately depends.

3

REPLY

JODY HEYMANN

I wrote "Can Working Families Ever Win?" to focus attention on the devastating magnitude of inequalities working families currently face in the United States and on the need to devote substantial collective efforts to addressing them. I am grateful for all the responses, and struck by the high degree of consensus they show on this fundamental issue.

Is it important that we as a nation do more to support the ability of parents to succeed at work and at caring for their children? This forum's participants responded with a near uniform: yes. There was strong agreement that meeting these needs should be one of our nation's highest priorities. Lotte Bailyn emphasizes that this "picture of the disconnect between current national and employment policies on the one hand and family needs for care on the other is a stark statement of what should be a critical national priority." James Comer writes that addressing this challenge is "as important as 'Homeland Security.'"

But while agreement on the need for change is an essential step, it is only the first. In this reply, I hope to move our discussion to the key next steps of debating policy design and strategies for change. Space constraints unfortunately will not permit me to discuss all of the important issues raised by each of the respondents. But I will address several themes that are likely to recur in public policy debates.

WHO IS AFFECTED THE MOST?

To put together the best policy solutions, we need to know which working families are most disadvantaged. But we also need to know how work-family issues affect the entire American public.

Addressing work-family issues is both particularly important and particularly difficult because of how they cut across two of our deepest social divides: gender and class. Because work-family issues were for too long seen as "women's issues" they were left in the backwater to ferment. Myra Ferree laments the continued emphasis that other authors place solely on women's roles instead of on changes in *men's and women's* lives. At the same time, Bailyn underscores the importance of keeping a critical perspective on how gender influences work and family. I agree with both points.

There is no doubt that women disproportionately bear the burden of our nation's failure to address the needs of working families. At the same time, to describe work-family issues as either women's responsibility or only affecting women would be grossly inaccurate.[1] Several essential points about the gender issue bear notice here.

As we enter the twenty-first century, the picture in the

United States is clear. Women do significantly more of the household chores (78 percent of women report that women carry more of this burden, as do 85 percent of men). Women are more likely than men to provide care for children, elderly parents, disabled adults, and children with disabilities or special needs. While women bear more of the caregiving burden, they face worse working conditions than men. They are less likely to have sick leave or vacation leave or to have any flexibility in the workplace. Moreover, a majority of the pay gap between women and men is associated with their differing family responsibilities.

Although women are disproportionately affected, America's failure to address the needs of working caregivers profoundly influences the daily lives of men as well. In any given week, 25 percent of men disrupt work to care for family members. Understanding the impact on both men and women is crucial for formulating fair policy and galvanizing the necessary political support.

The story about class is also more complex than is often portrayed. The complexity comes out in the responses in this forum. William Galston argues that the real problems are faced by families between 150 and 300 percent of the poverty line. And Karen Nussbaum writes that "the problems faced by families go far beyond the poor."

The findings of studies conducted by my research team support the contention that the problems, while most severe for the poor, are faced by families well beyond the poor and the near-poor. I have repeatedly interviewed low-income parents who have lost their jobs and others whose children have ended up in the hospital when they had to choose between keeping a job that put food on the table and caring for a sick child. Yet my research group has also frequently interviewed *middle-class* parents whose children have ended up in the emergency room from injuries sustained when they were left home alone, whose children with special needs are failing to get the support they need to make it through school, and who have lost jobs when they put meeting their children's essential needs above workplace demands.

The majority of middle-class families in the United States still cannot routinely rely on such basic benefits as paid leave during a family emergency. Yet, while the gaps affect families throughout American society, there is no doubt that low-income families face the starkest conditions. Getting these facts right is fundamental if we are to ensure that proposed policies narrow the chasms between families' needs and circumstances and between poor and affluent families.

Policy Responses

What does this picture of the impacts across social class mean for public policy? Galston argues for targeted and means-tested programs; Theda Skocpol and others for universal ones. There are strong arguments on both sides.

How should we decide when it comes to the question of whether work-family programs should be means-tested? I would argue we should answer at least three questions. First, which strategy will best help ensure that the needs of *all* working families are met? Second, which design will promote equal opportunity and not exacerbate existing inequalities? Third, what design is most likely to make a high-quality program feasible?

"Can Working Families Ever Win?" argues for the importance of a number of policy and programmatic initiatives. I will focus here on three key types: paid leave as an example of essential job benefits, preschool as an example of the value of expanding educational opportunities, and improved workplace culture as an example of the importance of institutional change.

Jodi Grant, Thomas Kochan, and Bailyn all underscore the importance of paid leave. Ensuring that all working Americans have paid leave could take a number of forms ranging from requiring employers to provide leave, to providing family leave insurance, to the more novel approach of flexible time accounts that Kochan recommends. In all cases, it only makes sense that these policies be universal. Universal standards are feasible; in fact, we have never implemented means-tested public policies regarding workplace standards. In this case, universality expresses the idea that all Americans have the right to decent working conditions. Even when implemented universally, new policies to ensure paid leave will disproportionately benefit low- and middle-income families—because they are currently the families that disproportionately lack reliable paid leave.

Both Comer and Isabelle Ferreras argue compellingly about the essential role of education. In the case of expanding both early education and programs for school-age children, I would argue that American children will have an equal opportunity to succeed at school only if the new programs are universal. Head Start, a means-tested program, is in its fourth decade. Yet despite its demonstrated importance, it still has not been funded to a level that provides access to most children living in poverty. In contrast, while inequalities that desperately need to be addressed remain in public K–12 education, they are far smaller than they would be in the absence of universal public schools.

Although we could rapidly make paid leave and early education universally available in the United States, as they are in other nations, we know less about how to bring other potential work-family changes to scale. Bailyn cogently raises the critical issue of one such area: workplace culture. While Bailyn and others have had a great deal of success with intensive interventions in individual workplaces, such interventions are unlikely to occur in the majority of the millions of American workplaces. If, for feasibility reasons, we must target this type of program, we should start where the conditions are worst and need is greatest: in low-wage workplaces.

There are many important aspects of policy design beyond the question of universality that there is not adequate space to discuss fully here. I would like to underscore the importance of at least four raised by respondents: Ferreras's litmus test for policies that support real "capabilities" and not just possibilities, Bradley Googin's attention to the realistic relationship between public and private sectors, Joan Tronto's concern that policy approaches should raise the value placed on caregiving, and Anne Alstott's reminder of the importance of programs for the nonworking poor.

POLITICS

The steps between policy proposal, passage, and implementation are many. I focused my original comments on the evidence regarding the condition of working families and not on the politics. However, I agree with respondents like Skocpol, who remind us that the politics on these issues are likely to be fierce. (Unfortunately, I am neither young enough nor innocent enough to believe that changes will follow as soon as we have documented the urgent needs of children and families.)

Consider two kinds of arguments we may see as the politics of work-family policy heats up: first, efforts to delegitimize any government role and second, efforts to assign all work-family problems to the sphere of individual responsibility. Skocpol is right to note that some conservatives seek to delegitimize "the very notion of nationally managed social provision." Jean Elshtain's response illustrates the point when she claims that providing better educational opportunities would make government "the nurturer of first resort." Clearly, providing early education will no more make government a nurturer of first resort than providing free public education during the past century and a half has done.

Elshtain also raises the individual responsibility debate when she argues by reference to her own immigrant family that if you work hard enough, everything will work out. It's nice to hear her family fared well, but none of us should assume that our personal lives are representative of the country as a whole. And, unfortunately, the evidence does not support Elshtain's contention that hers was a "typical American immigrant story." Indeed, four of five children of immigrants in the United States have not had the opportunity to complete college. In *Amazing Grace*, Jonathan Kozol eloquently describes the problem with generalizing from individual success stories: "The trouble with miracles, [however,] is that they don't happen for most children; and a good society cannot be built on miracles or on the likelihood that they will keep occurring."

While Elshtain is wrong on the facts, she will not be alone in making such arguments. Having the evidence to accurately counter them is important. However, that will not be enough. Translating the wide public support for work-family polices into broad-based political participation would make a substantial difference.

Nussbaum speaks compellingly about the critical role the labor movement might play in such efforts. Frances Fox Piven supports this call while expressing concern about some of the profound challenges labor currently faces in the United States. I agree with both and would only add that just as unions have a great deal to contribute to a campaign calling for our country to better address the needs of working families, unions also have a great deal to gain by taking on these issues. Union membership is down in the United States to 13.5 percent and unionization is particularly low in sectors in which women disproportionately work.

Ferree raises the possibility of a role for the women's movement in moving this agenda forward. As in the case of the unions, addressing the needs of working families may help this movement as much as the movement may help the agenda. The women's movement has become sadly fractured for many reasons, but one of the important reasons has been its inability to successfully articulate goals that support women who see one of their important roles as that of caregiver, whether or not they are also paid workers.

While there is little doubt that these movements can play critical roles in moving legislation forward, there is also no doubt that important legislative changes can be made with broad public support, even without mass movements. What else may make a difference? Among other factors, leadership matters more than we often credit. Universal preschool education passed in Georgia with a lottery and leadership but without a true statewide movement. Coalitions of organizations matter. The Family Medical Leave Act was passed without a mass movement. But it had strong support from organizations representing the elderly, disabled, and working women and men, and it had an organized coalition. Finally, bridging divides will matter. While some work-family proposals will split inevitably across political or labor-business divides, others need not, as the efforts of bipartisan groups at the state level and individuals like Donna Klein of the Employer Group demonstrate. We should harvest the fruits of this common ground.

A COMPELLING NEED

The consensus was nearly universal among the responses: we need to address the conditions faced by working families in the United States. We have to ensure that we meet the needs of families now living in or near poverty, while providing better supports to *all* families. Even Elshtain argues that "because we are all in it together, we cannot tolerate over the long haul, permanent and growing gaps in the ways of life the vast majority of Americans live and presume that the 'glue' will hold."

As founding director of the Project on Global Working Families, I lead a research team examining these issues not only in North America and Europe but also in Latin America, Africa, and Asia. The problems we have heard from families in Houston and Sacramento are echoed in Tegucigalpa and Gabarone. In the immediate future, we will need to address these issues as a national community. In the long run, as Susan Okin reminds us in her response, we will need to address these same issues as a global community.

NOTES

JODY HEYMANN / *Can Working Families Ever Win?*

This essay draws on *The Widening Gap: Why America's Working Families Are in Jeopardy and What Can Be Done about It*, by Jody Heymann (New York: Basic Books, 2000). The research was made possible by the generous support of the National Institute of Child Health and Human Development, the William T. Grant Foundation, and the Canadian Institute for Advanced Research. I am particularly grateful for the assistance of Alison Earle, Jennifer Eckerman, and Alyssa Rayman-Read in the preparation of this version.

1. Donald J. Hernandez and David E. Myers, *America's Children: Resources from Family, Government, and the Economy* (New York: Russell Sage Foundation, 1993).

2. Donald J. Hernandez, "Children's Changing Access to Resources: A Historical Perspective," in *Families in the U.S.: Kinship and Domestic Politics*, ed. Karen V. Hansen and Anita Ilta Garey (Philadelphia: Temple University Press, 1998), 201–15.

3. Ibid.

4. Alice Kessler-Harris, *Out to Work: A History of Wage-Earning Women in the United States* (New York: Oxford University Press, 1982).

5. Claudia Goldin, *Understanding the Gender Gap: An Economic History of American Women* (New York: Oxford University Press, 1990).

6. Before the war, for example, three out of five school districts refused to hire married women; after the war, only one out of five refused. Before the war, 50 percent of school districts fired women who married while employed; after the war, only 10 percent did. When the marriage bans eroded, the rise in wage labor by married women commenced in earnest.

7. Hernandez and Myers, *America's Children;* Bureau of the Census, *Statistical Abstract of the United States: 1998,* 118th ed. (Washington, D.C.: GPO, 1998).

8. Worker's compensation, the first of these to be enacted on a wide scale, had been adopted by ten states as of 1911 and by forty-two states as of 1920; all fifty states now have such laws. At a state level, California passed the first mandatory old-age assistance in 1929, and Wisconsin adopted the first compulsory unemployment insurance in 1932; see Phyllis J. Day, *A New History of Social Welfare* (Boston: Allyn & Bacon, 1997). The Social Security Act of 1935 turned income support for the elderly and unemployment insurance into federal policies and programs.

9. Readers may wish to refer to Jody Heymann, *The Widening Gap: Why America's Working Families Are in Jeopardy and What Can Be Done About It* (New York: Basic Books, 2000), for analysis of a range of related issues: gender disparities, outdated working conditions and practices, the care of elderly and disabled family members, and the role of extended family in providing support.

10. Janet Currie and Duncan Thomas, "Does Head Start Make a Difference?" *American Economic Review* 85 (1995): 341–64.

11. Ruth McKey, Larry Condell, Harriet Ganson, Barbara Barrett, Catherine McConkey, and Margaret Plantz, *The Impact of Head Start on Children, Families, and Communities: Final Report of the Head Start Evaluation, Synthesis, and Utilization Project* (Washington, D.C.: CSR Inc., 1985); Susan Ring Andrews, Janet Blumenthal, Dale Johnson, Alfred Kahn, Carol Ferguson, Thomas Lasater, Paul Malone, and Doris Wallace, "The Skills of Mothering: A Study of Parent Child Development Centers," *Monographs of the Society for Research in Child Development* 47 (1982): 1–83; W. Steven Barnett, "Long-Term Effects of Early Childhood Programs on Cognitive and School Outcomes," *The Future of Children* 5 (1995): 25–50; Frances Campbell and Craig Ramey, "Effects of Early Intervention on Intellectual and Academic Achievement: A Follow-Up Study of Children from Low-Income Families," *Child Development* 65 (1994): 684–98; Howard Garber, *The Milwaukee Project: Preventing Mental Retardation in Children at Risk* (Washington, D.C.: American Association on Mental Retardation, 1988); Dale Johnson and Todd Walker, "A Follow-Up Evaluation of the Houston Parent-Child

Development Center: School Performance," *Journal of Early Intervention* 15 (1991): 226–36.

12. Karen Shulman, *Issue Brief: The High Cost of Child Care Puts Quality Care Out of Reach for Many Families: Children's Defense Fund* (Washington, D.C.: Children's Defense Fund, 2000).

13. Craig Turner, Head Start Bureau, in a telephone interview by Maria Palacios, 7 March 2000, based on *Head Start Program Information Report* (September 1998–June 1999) and data from Head Start Bureau databases.

14. Jill Posner and Deborah Lowe Vandell, "Low-Income Children's After-School Care: Are There Beneficial Effects of After-School Programs?" *Child Development* 65 (1994): 440–56; Department of Education, *Safe and Smart: Making After-School Hours Work for Kids* (Washington, D.C., 1998). Available at http://www.ed.gov/pubs/SafeandSmart [6 July 2000].

15. Catherine E. Snow, *Preventing Reading Difficulties in Young Children* (Washington, D.C.: National Research Council and National Academy of Sciences, 1998).

16. Darrell Morris, Beverly Shaw, and Jan Perney, "Helping Low Readers in Grades 2 and 3: An After-School Volunteer Tutoring Program," *Elementary School Journal* 91 (1990): 133–50.

17. Jean L. Richardson, Kathleen Dwyer, Kimberly McGuigan, William B. Hansen, Clyde W. Dent, C. Anderson Johnson, Steven Y. Sussman, Bonnie Brannon, and BrianFlay, "Substance Abuse among Eighth-Grade Students Who Take Care of Themselves after School," *Pediatrics* 84 (1989): 556–66; D. Blyth, and N. Leffert, "Communities as Contexts for Adolescent Development: An Empirical Analysis," *Journal of Adolescent Research* 10 (1995): 64–87.

18. James Allen Fox and Sanford A. Newman, *After-School Crime or After-School Programs: Tuning in the Prime Time for Violent Juvenile Crime and Implications for National Policy* (Washington, D.C.: Fight Crime Invest in Kids, 1997); Stephen P. Schinke, Mario A. Orlandi, and Kristin L. Cole, "Boys and Girls Clubs in Public Housing Developments: Prevention Services for Youth at Risk," *Journal of Community Psychology,* OSAP special issue, 1992; Department of Education, *Safe and Smart.*

19. Melissa Sickmund, Howard N. Snyder, and Eileen Poe-Yamagata, *Juvenile Offenders and Victims: 1997 Update on Violence,* report

prepared for the Department of Justice, Office of Juvenile Justice and Delinquency Prevention (Washington, D.C., 1997).

20. Department of Education, *Safe and Smart.*

21. General Accounting Office, *Welfare Reform: Implications of Increased Work Participation for Child Care* (Washington, D.C., 1997).

22. Robert Bradley, Stephen L. Rock, Bettye M. Caldwell, Pandia T. Harris, and Holly M. Hamrick, "Home Environment and School Performance among Black Elementary School Children," *Journal of Negro Education* 56 (1987): 499–509; Barbara K. Iverson, Geraldine D. Brownlee, and Herbert J. Walberg, "Parent-Teacher Contacts and Student Learning," *Journal of Educational Research* 74 (1981): 394–96; David L. Stevenson and David P. Baker, "The Family-School Relation and the Child's School Performance," *Child Development* 58 (1987): 1348–57.

23. Timothy Z. Keith, Patricia B. Keith, Gretchen C. Troutman, Patricia G. Bickley, Paul S. Trivette, and Kusum Singh, "Does Parental Involvement Affect Eighth-Grade Student Achievement? Structural Analysis of National Data," *School Psychology Review* 22 (1993): 474–76; Paul G. Fehrmann, Timothy Z. Keith, and Thomas M. Reimers, "Home Influences on School Learning: Direct and Indirect Effects of Parental Involvement on High School Grades," *Journal of Educational Research* 80 (1987): 330–37.

24. Arthur J. Reynolds, "Comparing Measures of Parental Involvement and Their Effects on Academic Achievement," *Early Childhood Research Quarterly* 7 (1992): 441–62; James Griffith, "Relation of Parental Involvement, Empowerment, and School Traits to Student Academic Performance," *Journal of Educational Research* 90 (1996): 33–41; Sandra L. Christenson, Theresa Rounds, and Deborah Gorney, "Family Factors and Student Achievement: An Avenue to Increase Students' Success," *School Psychology Quarterly* 7 (1992): 178–206; D. Miller and M. Kelley, "Interventions for Improving Homework Performance: A Critical Review," *School Psychology Quarterly* 6 (1991): 174–85; James P. Comer, "Home-School Relationships as They Affect the Academic Success of Children," *Education and Urban Society* 16 (1984): 323–37; John W. Fantuzzo, Gwendolyn Y. Davis, and Marika D. Ginsburg, "Effects of Parental Involvement in Isolation or in Combination with Peer Tutoring on Student Self-Concept and Mathematics Achievement," *Journal of Educational Psychology* 87 (1995): 272–81.

25. Inger Kristensson-Hallstrom, Gunnel Elander, and Gerhard

Malmfors, "Increased Parental Participation on a Pediatric Surgical Daycare Unit," *Journal of Clinical Nursing* 6 (1997): 297–302; P. R. Mahaffy, "The Effects of Hospitalization on Children Admitted for Tonsillectomy and Adenoidectomy," *Nursing Research* 14 (1965): 12–19; John Bowlby, *Child Care and the Growth of Love* (Baltimore: Penguin Books, 1965); James Robertson, *Young Children in Hospitals* (New York: Basic Books, 1958); Sarah J. Palmer, "Care of Sick Children by Parents: A Meaningful Role," *Journal of Advanced Nursing* 18 (1993): 185–91; G. van der Schyff, "The Role of Parents during Their Child's Hospitalization," *Australian Nurses Journal* 8 (1979): 57–58, 61.

26. M. R. Taylor and P. O'Connor, "Resident Parents and Shorter Hospital Stay," *Archives of Disease in Childhood* 64 (1989): 274–76.

27. S. Jody Heymann, Sara Toomey, and Frank Furstenberg, "Working Parents: What Factors Are Involved in Their Ability to Take Time Off from Work When Their Children Are Sick?" *Archives of Pediatrics and Adolescent Medicine* 153 (1999): 870–74.

28. S. Jody Heymann, Alison Earle, and Brian Egleston, "Parental Availability for the Care of Sick Children," *Pediatrics* 98 (1996): 226–30; Heymann, Toomey, and Furstenberg, "Working Parents"; S. Jody Heymann and Alison Earle, "The Impact of Welfare Reform on Parents' Ability to Care for Their Children's Health," *American Journal of Public Health* 89 (1999): 502–5.

29. Heymann and Earle, "Impact of Welfare Reform"; Heymann, Toomey, and Furstenberg, "Working Parents"; Heymann, Earle, and Egleston, "Parental Availability."

30. Women, Infants, and Children (WIC) is a program providing education, nutritional supplementation, and access to health services for low-income, pregnant, and breastfeeding women and those with preschool children.

31. Janet Gornick and Marcia Meyers, *Early Childhood Education and Care (ECEC): Cross-National Variation in Service Organization and Financing* (New York: Columbia Institute for Child and Family Policy, 2000).

32. Department of Education, National Center for Education Statistics, table 55–4: "Expenditures per Student for Early Childhood Education, 1993." Available at http://nces.ed.gov/pubs/ce/c97p55.pdf [11 July 2000].

33. Urban Institute, *Children's Budget Report: A Detailed Analysis of*

Spending on Low-Income Children's Programs in Thirteen States (Washington, D.C.: Urban Institute, 1998).

34. David and Lucile Packard Foundation, *The Future of Children: Caring for Infants and Toddlers* (Los Altos, Calif.: The David and Lucile Packard Foundation, 2001).

35. Gornick and Meyers, *Early Childhood Education and Care.*

36. Department of Education, National Center for Education Statistics, table 39: "Historical Summary of Public Elementary and Secondary School Statistics: 1869–70 to 1996–97." Available at http://nces.ed.gov/npubs2000/digest99/d99t039.html [11 July 2000].

37. Ibid.

38. Department of Education, Twentieth-first Century Community Learning Centers. Available at http://www.ed.gov/ 21stcclc/index.html [14 June 2001].

39. Bureau of the Census, *Resident Populations Estimates of the United States by Age and Sex: April 1, 1990, to July 1, 1999, with Short-Term Projection to November 1, 2000.* Available at http://www.census.gov/population/estimates/nation/intfile2–1.txt [2 January 2001].

40. Department of Education, National Center for Education Statistics, *Digest of Education Statistics 1997*, NCES 98–015 (Washington, D.C., 1997).

41. Judith Treas and Ramon Torrecilha, "The Older Population," in *State of the Union: America in the 1990s*, vol. 2, *Social Trends*, ed. R. Farley (New York: Russell Sage Foundation), 47–92.

42. United Nations, Department of Economic and Social Development, Statistics Division, *Demographic Yearbook 1991* (New York: United Nations, 1992).

43. Bureau of the Census, *1990 Census of Population and Housing: Social, Economic, and Housing Characteristics* (Washington D. C., 1992).

44. Lisa F. Berkman, "The Relationship of Social Networks and Social Support to Morbidity and Mortality," in *Social Support and Health,* ed. Sheldon Cohen and S. Leonard Syme (Orlando: Academic Press, 1985), 241–62; Lisa F. Berkman, Thomas E. Oxman, and Teresa E. Seeman, "Social Networks and Social Support among the Elderly: Assessment Issues," in *The Epidemiologic Study of the Elderly,* ed. Robert B. Wallace and Robert F. Woolson (New York: Oxford University Press), 196–212; Lisa F. Berkman and S. Leonard Syme, "Social Networks, Host

Resistance and Mortality: A Nine-Year Follow-Up Study of Alameda County Residents," in *Psychosocial Processes in Health: A Reader,* ed. Andrew Steptoe and Jan Wardle (Cambridge: Cambridge University Press, 1994), vii–11.

45. International Labour Organization, *Maternity Protection at Work: Revision of the Maternity Protection Convention (Revised), 1952 (No. 103), and Recommendation, 1952 (No. 95) Report V(1)* (Geneva: International Labour Office, 1997).

ANNE ALSTOTT / *Limited Options*

1. By "liberal-egalitarian," I mean the strand of liberal philosophy represented by, among others, John Rawls, Bruce Ackerman, Ronald Dworkin, and Philippe Van Parijs.

2. Barbara Bergmann, *Saving Our Children From Poverty: What the U.S. Can Learn from France* (New York: Russell Sage, 1996).

3. This does not imply, of course, that every parent should sit at home for eighteen years. Parents can meet children's routine needs by themselves or with paid help, but parents must be prepared to drop their own plans when a child's illness, accident, or developmental crisis occurs. To do otherwise would be neglectful.

4. Bureau of the Census, *Fertility of American Women: June 2000* (Washington D.C., 2001), table 4. These data are for mothers, aged fifteen to forty-four, whether married or unmarried, excluding mothers of infants, who work much less. Although Heymann is correct that more than 70 percent of mothers are *in the labor force,* a significant percentage work part time.

5. Ibid. Families with a yearly income of less than $10,000 have the smallest percentage of full-time working mothers and the highest rate of maternal unemployment.

6. The great majority of Americans from *every income class* prefer to have one parent take time out of the paid workforce to care for young children. See *Caring for Infants and Toddlers* (2001), at http://www.futureofchildren.org/information__show.htm? doc__id=80499; see also information from an ICR/ *Washington Post* poll, reported in "Child Care: A Nation Divided?" at http://www.publicagenda.org/issues/nation__divided__detail.cfm?issue__type=childcare&list=2

7. Combined with FMLA, which ensures unpaid leave, such a program would, de facto, provide paid leave for workers while also offering support to nonworking and single-earner families.

8. Most obviously, these proposals raise questions about work incentives, social waste, and the justification for redistribution to parents. For some answers, see Bruce Ackerman and Anne Alstott, *The Stakeholder Society* (New Haven, Conn.: Yale University Press, 1999); and Anne Alstott, "Work vs. Freedom: A Liberal Challenge to Employment Subsidies," *Yale Law Journal* 108 (1999): 967. I advocate redistribution to caretakers in my new book, tentatively titled *No Exit: Justice for Caretakers*.

JOAN TRONTO / *The Value of Care*

1. Mona Harrington makes an argument about how care creates gender inequality in *Care and Equality* (New York: Knopf, 1999). Eva Kittay shows how caring for the dependent requires a rethinking of the nature of equality in *Love's Labor: Essays on Women, Equality, and Dependence* (New York: Routledge, 1999).

2. Heymann's example that government agencies have been slow to respond to the different temporal needs of citizens who engage in care is a powerful one. In Italy, feminists have worked to reform local governments so that they are attentive to *tempi della città*.

3. See Margaret Urban Walker, "Getting Out of Line: Alternatives to Life as a Career," in *Mother Time: Women, Aging, and Ethics*, ed. M. Walker (Lanham, Md.: Rowman and Littlefield, 1999).

4. This distinction is Kari Waerness's; see her "Informal and Formal Care in Old Age: What Is Wrong With the New Ideology in Scandinavia Today?" in *Gender and Caring: Work and Welfare in Britain and Scandinavia*, ed. Clare Ungerson (London: Harvester, Wheatsheaf, 1990).

JAMES P. COMER / *The Place of Education*

1. James P. Comer, *Waiting for a Miracle: Why Schools Can't Solve Our Problems and How We Can* (New York: Dutton, 1997).

2. Daniel Goleman, *Emotional Intelligence* (New York: Bantam, 1995).

3. Harold G. Vatter, *The Drive to Industrial Maturity: The U.S. Econ-*

omy, 1860–1914 (Westport, Conn.: Greenwood Press, 1975); Harold G. Vatter and John F. Walker, eds., *History of the U.S. Economy since World War II* (New York: M. E. Sharpe, 1996); David C. Mowery and Nathan Rosenberg, *Paths of Innovation: Technological Change in Twentieth-Century America* (New York: Cambridge University Press, 1998).

4. James P. Comer, *School Power: Implications of an Intervention Project* (New York: Free Press; London: Collier Macmillan, 1980).

5. James P. Comer, "Schools That Develop Children," *The American Prospect*, 23 April 2001.

THEDA SKOCPOL / *The Political Bind*

1. See Theda Skocpol and Richard C. Leone, *The Missing Middle: Working Families and the Future of American Social Policy* (New York: Norton, 2001).

LOTTE BAILYN / *Adding Gender and Work*

1. Mona Harrington, *Care and Equality: Inventing a New Family Politics* (New York: Knopf, 1999); Joan Williams, *Unbending Gender: Why Family and Work Conflict and What to Do about It* (New York: Oxford University Press, 2000); *Integrating Work and Family Life: A Holistic Approach* (Cambridge: MIT Sloan School of Management, 2001).

2. Heymann's useful discussion, in her book, of gender inequalities is a beginning to such a theory-based analysis of gender.

3. See Rhona Rapoport, Lotte Bailyn, Joyce K. Fletcher, and Bettye H. Pruitt, *Beyond Work-Family Balance: Advancing Gender Equity and Workplace Performance* (San Francisco: Jossey-Bass, 2002).

ISABELLE FERRERAS / *Beyond Opportunity*

1. Amartya Sen observes that there are "systematic disparities in the freedoms men and woman enjoy in different societies, and these disparities are often not reducible to differences in income and resources." See *Inequality Reexamined* (Cambridge: Harvard University Press, 1992), 122. Regarding inequality between men and women in Western socie-

ties, one of the main challenges is to make sense of why people (think of men and women) with the same amount of resources may still find themselves with very different real choices when it comes to orienting their lives in accordance with their own desires.

2. For more on this, see Jean De Munck and Isabelle Ferreras, "Collective Rights, Deliberation, and Capabilities," in *Towards a European Politics of Capabilities?* ed. Robert Salais and Robert Villeneuve, forthcoming.

Thomas Kochan / *The Right Time*

1. These comments build on ideas developed in two recent works: Paul Osterman, Thomas Kochan, Richard Locke, and Michael Piore, *Working in America: A Blueprint for the Labor Market* (Cambridge: MIT Press, 2001); and Lotte Bailyn, Robert Drago, and Thomas Kochan, *Integrating Work and Family Life: A Holistic Approach* (Cambridge: MIT Sloan School of Management, 2001).

Myra Marx Ferree / *Sharing the Burden*

1. Christine Bose, *Women in 1900: Gateway to the Political Economy of the Twentieth Century* (Philadelphia: Temple University Press, 2001).

2. Mary P. Ryan, *Cradle of the Middle Class: The Family in Oneida County, N.Y., 1790–1865* (New York: Cambridge University Press, 1983).

3. An excellent example of both calling for social support and explicitly blaming feminists for failing to have obtained it can be seen in Sylvia Hewlett, *A Lesser Life: The Myth of Women's Liberation in America* (New York: Warner Books, 1987).

4. See, for example, Elisabeth Clemens, *The People's Lobby: Organizational Innovation and the Rise of Interest Group Politics in the United States, 1890–1925* (Chicago: University of Chicago Press, 1997). For analysis of *why* the United States lacks the social supports that families in Europe enjoy, see Gwendolyn Mink, *The Wages of Motherhood: Inequality in the Welfare State, 1917–1942* (Ithaca, N.Y.: Cornell University Press, 1995).

Jodi Grant / *Affordable Policies*

1. Department of Labor, *Balancing the Needs of Families and Employers: Family and Medical Leave Surveys, 2000 Update,* a survey conducted

by Westat (Washington, D.C., 2000). Available at http://www.dol.gov/dol/asp/public/fmla/main.htm.

2. Ibid.

3. Jane Waldfogel, "International Policies toward Parental Leave and Child Care," *The Future of Children* 11 (spring/summer 2001).

4. Department of Labor, *Balancing the Needs of Families and Employers.*

5. Heymann, *The Widening Gap.*

6. Bureau of the Census, *Maternity Leave and Employment Patterns: 1961–1995,* a study by Kristin Smith, Barbara Downs, and Martin O'Connell (Washington, D.C., 2001).

7. Waldfogel, "International Policies."

8. International Labour Organization, *Conditions of Work Digest, on Maternity and Work* (Geneva: ILO, 1994). Available at www.ilo.org.

9. Ibid.

10. Congressional Commission on Family and Medical Leave, *A Workable Balance: Report to Congress on Family and Medical Leave Policies* (Washington, D.C., 1996).

11. Bureau of the Census, *Maternity Leave and Employment Patterns.*

12. Congressional Commission on Family and Medical Leave, *A Workable Balance.*

13. Bureau of Labor Statistics, "Unemployment Rate—Civilian Labor Force," Labor Force Statistics from the Current Population Survey, Series ID: LFU21000000. Available at www.bls.gov.

14. Zero to Three: The National Center for Infants, Toddlers, and Families, Civitas, and the Brio Corporation, *What Grown-Ups Understand about Child Development: A National Benchmark Survey,* conducted by DYG, Inc., October 2000.

15. National Family Caregivers Association, NFCA Caregiver Survey, July 2000. Available at www.nfcacares.org.

16. National Partnership for Women and Families, *Family Matters,* a survey conducted by Lake, Sosin, Snell, Perry & Associates, Inc., 1998.

17. Bureau of the Census, *Maternity Leave and Employment Patterns.*

JODY HEYMANN / *Reply*

1. For a more complete discussion, see Heymann, *The Widening Gap.*

ABOUT THE CONTRIBUTORS

ANNE ALSTOTT is professor of law at Yale Law School. She is coauthor with Bruce Ackerman of *The Stakeholder Society* and author of the forthcoming *No Exit: Justice for Caretakers.*

LOTTE BAILYN is professor of management at MIT's Sloan School and author of *Breaking the Mold: Women, Men, and Time in the New Corporate World.*

JOSHUA COHEN is professor of philosophy and political science and Goldberg Professor of the Humanities at the Massachusetts Institute of Technology. He is editor in chief of *Boston Review* and author of numerous books and articles on political theory.

JAMES P. COMER is Maurice Falk Professor of Child Psychiatry at the Yale University Child Study Center. He founded the center's School Development Program in 1968.

JEAN BETHKE ELSHTAIN is professor of social and political ethics at the University of Chicago and author of *Jane Addams and the Dream of American Democracy.*

MYRA MARX FERREE teaches sociology at the University of Wisconsin and is coauthor of *Shaping Abortion Discourse: Democracy and the Public Sphere in Germany and the United States.*

ISABELLE FERRERAS is research fellow of the National Fund for Scientific Research in the department of political and social sciences at Université catholique de Louvain in Belgium.

WILLIAM A. GALSTON is professor at the University of Maryland's School of Public Affairs and former deputy assistant to President Clinton for domestic policy.

BRADLEY K. GOOGINS is executive director of the Center for Corporate Citizenship and teaches at the Wallace E. Carroll School of Management at Boston College.

ABOUT THE CONTRIBUTORS

JODI GRANT is director of Work and Family Programs and Public Policy for the National Partnership for Women and Families.

JODY HEYMANN is on the faculty at Harvard University, chairs the Work, Family, and Democracy Initiative, and is founding director of the Project on Global Working Families.

THOMAS A. KOCHAN teaches at the Sloan School of Management and codirects both the MIT Institute for Work and Employment Research and the MIT Workplace Center.

KAREN NUSSBAUM directs the AFL-CIO's Working Women's Department and directed the Women's Bureau in the Labor Department during the first Clinton administration.

SUSAN MOLLER OKIN is professor of ethics and political science at Stanford University and author of *Is Multiculturalism Bad for Women?*

FRANCES FOX PIVEN teaches at CUNY Graduate Center and is coauthor with Richard A. Cloward of *Regulating the Poor, Poor Peoples' Movements,* and *Why Americans Still Don't Vote.*

JOEL ROGERS is professor of law, political science, and sociology at the University of Wisconsin; a member of the *Boston Review* editorial board; and author of numerous articles and books on American politics.

THEDA SKOCPOL is professor of government and sociology at Harvard University, directs the Center for American Political Studies, and is president of the American Political Science Association.

JOAN TRONTO is professor of political science and women's studies at CUNY and author of *Moral Boundaries: A Political Argument for an Ethic of Care.*